MINING RAILWAYS
OF THE KLONDIKE

NARROW GAUGE RAILWAYS
SERVING COAL MINES ON CLIFF CREEK
AND COAL CREEK, AND A
PLACER GOLD OPERATION ON BEAR CREEK,
YUKON TERRITORY

1899 TO 1918

Mining Railways of the Klondike

NARROW GAUGE RAILWAYS
SERVING COAL MINES ON CLIFF CREEK
AND COAL CREEK, AND A
PLACER GOLD OPERATION
ON BEAR CREEK, YUKON TERRITORY

1899 TO 1918

by
Eric L. Johnson

Editing and Layout by
Lorne H. Nicklason

PACIFIC COAST DIVISION, INC
CANADIAN RAILROAD HISTORICAL ASSOCIATION
January, 1995

Published by:

Pacific Coast Division Inc.

Canadian Railroad Historical Association
P.O. Box 1006, Station A
Vancouver, B.C. V6C 2P1

Canadian Cataloguing in Publication Data:

Johnson, Eric L. (Eric Lennart), 1933-
    Mining railways of the Klondike

(B.C. rail guide ; no. 13)

1. Railroads-Yukon Territory-History. 2. Mineral industries-Yukon Territory-History.
I. Canadian Railroad Historical Association. Pacific Coast Division. II Title. III. Series.
HE2809.Y9J63 1995   385'.54'097191   C95-910201-9

ISBN 0-9697633-4-4

Printed by:
    Friesen Printers
    Altona, Manitoba

Other BC Rail Guides currently available:

No.8   **The CPR's English Bay Branch**,
               by David Ll. Davies and Lorne Nicklason, 1993
No. 10   **The Britannia Copper Mine Railway**,
               by David Davies, 1991
No. 11   **Industrial Locomotives**,
               by Mervyn T. 'Mike' Green, 1992
No. 12   **Railroading in British Columbia:**
             A Bibliography,
               by Ron H. Meyer, 1993

TABLE OF CONTENTS

ACKNOWLEDGEMENTS..viii

INTRODUCTION x
The Klondike Mines Railway..xii

Chapter 1 - THREE CREEKS WITH THREE RAILWAYS..........1

Chapter 2 - THE RAILWAY ON CLIFF CREEK 6

Chapter 3 - THE RAILWAY ON COAL CREEK - PART I.......17

Chapter 4 - THE RAILWAY ON COAL CREEK - PART II......30

Chapter 5 - THE RAILWAY ON BEAR CREEK........................48

APPENDICES
    A) LOCOMOTIVES OF THE MINING RAILWAYS......62
    B) EQUIPMENT AND FREIGHT CARS OF THE
        MINING RAILWAYS 73
    C) LOCOMOTIVES OF THE KLONDIKE
        MINES RAILWAY...75
    D) CHRONOLOGY...76

MAPS

THE YUKON TERRITORY vii
THE KLONDIKE DISTRICT 2
CLIFF CREEK AND COAL CREEK 8
BEAR CREEK AND THE KLONDIKE RIVER 50

LOCOMOTIVE PROFILES

THE TWO CCCCo 0-6-0T
      PORTER LOCOMOTIVES 62, 64
THE NAT&TCo 0-4-0T PORTER LOCOMOTIVE 66
THE DYMCo 0-4-0T PORTER LOCOMOTIVES 68
THE NLP&CCo LIMA SHAY LOCOMOTIVE..........................72

LIST OF ACRONYMS

CCCCo	Coal Creek Coal Company
CKMCo	Canadian Klondyke Mining Company
DEL&PCo	Dawson Electric Light and Power Company
D&WHNCo	Dawson and White Horse Navigation Company
DYMCo	Detroit Yukon Mining Company
KMR	Klondike Mines Railway
NAT&TCo	North American Transportation and Trading Company
NLP&CCo	Northern Light, Power and Coal Company
WP&YR	White Pass and Yukon Route
YCGC	Yukon Consolidated Gold Corporation
YGCo	Yukon Gold Company

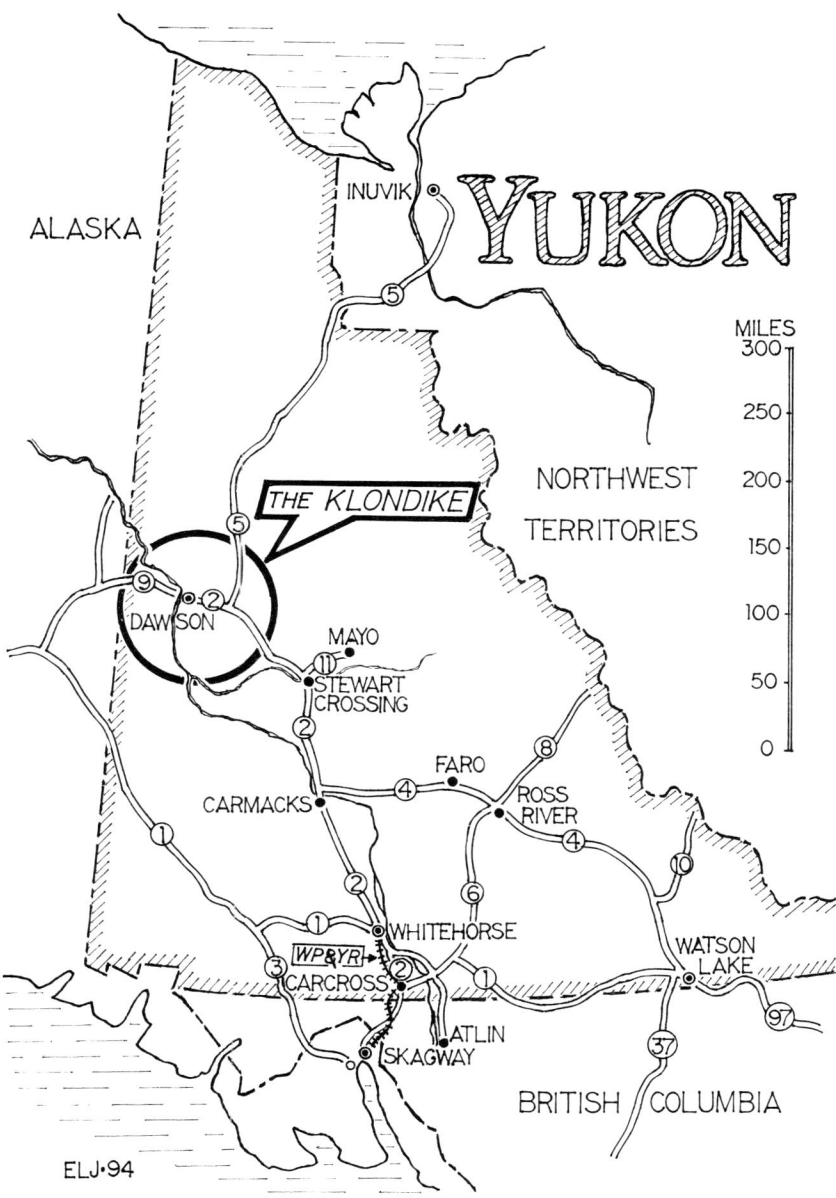

ACKNOWLEDGEMENTS

Almost no business records of the companies which operated the mining railways of the Klondike, from 1899 until 1918, survive today, hence for this story it was necessary to resort to microfilmed copies of Klondike newspapers. In the early days of the Klondike boom, gold made all the headlines, whereas little attention was paid to the coal mines being developed and their associated railways. In the few events reported, serious factual discrepancies are sometimes seen, requiring some interpretation. Newspapers scanned for information were: the Dawson Daily News, the Klondike Nugget, the Yukon Sun, the Dawson Record, and the Yukon World.

Among many individuals who contributed to this story are: Keith A. Christenson, Harry Cooper, Robert G. Hilton, Ken Hynek, George R. Kadelak, Don A. Marenzi, Bob Mitchell, Gunnar Nilsson, and Gregory Skuce.

Organizations from which photos and data were received are:
Alaska State Library, Juneau, Alaska
British Columbia Archives and Records Service, Victoria, B.C.
Dawson City Museum, Dawson, Yukon
Friends of the Tanana Valley Railroad, Inc., Fairbanks, Alaska
Museum of History and Industry, Seattle, Washington
National Archives of Canada, Ottawa, Ontario
Omak Public Library, Omak, Washington
Parks Canada, Winnipeg, Manitoba, and Whitehorse, Yukon
University of Alaska, Fairbanks, Alaska

University of British Columbia, Vancouver, British Columbia
University of Washington Libraries, Seattle, Washington
Vancouver Public Library, Vancouver, British Columbia
Yukon Archives, Whitehorse, Yukon

Publications from which information was also gathered are:

Walter R. Curtin	Yukon Voyage, 1938
Lewis H. Green	The Gold Hustlers, 1977
Mervyn T. Green	Industrial Locomotives, 1992
John E. Lewis	Reservation Narrow Gauge, 1980
Don A. Marenzi	Narrow Gauge and Short Line Gazette, pp. 34-37, May-June, 1982
Bob Mitchell	Report on the Cultural Resources at Coal Creek, 1992
Government of Canada	
	Canada Gazette, 1899 to 1909
	Geological Survey of Canada, Bulletins and Memoirs, 1898 to 1912
	List of Shipping, 1898 to 1920
	Sessional Papers, 1898 to 1910

INTRODUCTION

Reposing in museums and private collections in the Yukon, British Columbia, and Alaska today are six small Porter saddle-tank, 36-inch gauge, locomotives. All are known to have worked in the Klondike district of the Yukon Territory in the early part of the 1900s, but their part in development of the Klondike has been forgotten over the years. In total, eight locomotives (two no longer exist) were brought to the district between 1899 and 1909 for use on three different mining railways. There has been some connection made between these industrial locomotives and the Klondike Mines Railway (KMR), also a 36-inch gauge railway, since one of the Porter locomotives, DYMCo (Detroit Yukon Mining Company) No. 4, is presently parked in the Dawson Museum alongside KMR engines Nos. 1, 2, and 3. But the numbering sequence is only coincidental - the KMR and DYMCo were separate business organizations.

The name "Klondike Mines" suggests the KMR was also a mining railway, but this was not so. The KMR was classed a "common carrier", granted a charter by the Government of Canada, and thus obligated to offer its services to any and all customers, carrying passengers and hauling freight and express for many industries and businesses. In contrast to a common carrier is an industrial railway which is restricted by law to servicing only its owner's own businesses; such was the case with the three mining railways of the Klondike - two built by coal mining companies, and the third by a

It is June, 1904, in Skagway, as four 7-ton Porter locomotives bought by the Detroit Yukon Mining Company start out by rail, and later by river, on the White Pass and Yukon Route to the Klondike. At Bear Creek, they would work for a few months on placer gold claims, and then be side-lined for only occasional jobs thereafter.

Vancouver Public Library, 9778

gold mining company. All three mining railways were in operation before the KMR began business. The histories of the locomotives of the KMR are well known since all operated at one time or another on the well-documented railway of the White Pass and Yukon Route, but the histories of the Porter saddle-tankers have never been adequately described. Various publications have speculated on the origins and purposes of the locomotives, but in

general have been in error. In fact nothing has been published
about two of the operations since the period before World War I.

THE KLONDIKE MINES RAILWAY

Since the stories of the mining railways interrelate in some ways
with the story of the Klondike Mines Railway, a short description of
this railway, and of its origins, is in order.

The discovery of rich gold-bearing gravel on Bonanza Creek,
Yukon Territory, in August of 1896 precipitated the great Klondike
gold rush. From a few hundred prospectors and miners then in the
Yukon, the non-native population rose to over 30,000 by 1900.
Transportation and freighting into the goldfield was an enormous
problem, and roads and trails - initially non-existent - were built
only after some time and many difficulties. Several speculators
applied to the federal government to be allowed to build railways
into the heart of the goldfield, but only one group gained a
franchise.

In 1899 the Parliament of Canada granted a charter in the name of
the Klondike Mines Railway (KMR) to a consortium of businessmen and speculators; the railway would be built from Klondike City
and Dawson City, Yukon Territory, river boat shipping ports on the
Yukon River, through the center of the Klondike goldfield, and on
to the Stewart River country. Among the charter members was
Harold Buchanan McGiverin, a very influential Ottawa lawyer, and
Thomas William O'Brien, a bona fide sourdough and owner or part-
owner of a number of Klondike City and Dawson City businesses.
O'Brien did his best to promote early completion of the railway, but
the charter languished for some years as the other, eastern
Canadian, members made little headway. A survey for the route of
the railway was first made in 1899, but it was not until 1902 that

Erastus Corning Hawkins, formerly with the White Pass and Yukon Route, took on the job of promoting the KMR.

Hawkins brought the KMR's first locomotive to Klondike City in September of 1902, but it was parked here on temporary trackage, laying idle until 1905. Hawkins had great difficulty in trying to attract backers for construction of the railway - something like a million dollars was needed. In Hawkins' own words, the name of the company, Klondike Mines Railway, was the greatest hindrance to his efforts. Investors associated the name with hundreds of fraudulent Klondike mining ventures which had proved valueless, but in mid-1904 Hawkins finally found financing in two British shipping magnates. Robert Lawther and John Latta provided the necessary cash and became almost sole owners of the Klondike Mines Railway. It was probably much to Hawkins' relief as he left the Klondike, never to return.

In the spring of 1905 engine No. 1 was finally fired up, and construction of the railway grade up the bed of Bonanza Creek began in earnest. (By this time, the mining railways of the Klondike had already been operating for six years.) But by late June, injunctions granted mining companies stalled grading crews - the companies objected to the right-of-way crossing their claims. After some delay, the courts ordered the railway to survey a new grade along the banks of the creek, and to compensate claim-owners where the right-of-way interfered with mining operations. By the time all was settled, fall had arrived in the Yukon Territory, and no further construction was done that year. However, new rolling stock for the railway had been ordered, and box cars and flat cars began arriving in September. Just before the shipping season on the Yukon River closed, engine No. 2 arrived.

A new contractor began work in March of 1906. Over the winter, Tom O'Brien and partner John Mackenzie had been awarded the contract to complete the railway. Although eight miles of grade had been finished by the previous contractor, only four miles were available following injunction settlements. By early July, rail was complete to Grand Forks, thirteen miles from Dawson, and by early October construction ceased with rail laid to Sulphur Springs, thirty-one miles from Dawson. At this time engine No. 3 was delivered to Klondike City where the railway's shops and round-house were located.

Plans were to continue construction next spring, south-easterly to the Stewart River country. But the volume of business handled by the railway, once in operation in late October of 1906, came as a bitter shock. Operating over the winter months, trains carried few passengers and little freight; business was a small fraction of the levels projected in Hawkins' prospectus of 1902. It was readily apparent to most that the railway should never have been built at this late stage in the development of the Klondike.

Gold production in the goldfield peaked between 1898 and 1900, and the federal government had in this time already built good roads into all the major mining camps. By 1903 the Klondike was in eclipse; the richest of gold claims had been worked out, population was declining, and numerous small mining operations were just beginning to be consolidated for exploitation by a few labour-efficient dredges. On Bonanza Creek were a few businesses which appreciated the coming of the railway, but beyond Grand Forks the line climbed away from the valley bottom, following ridges to the Sulphur Springs terminal; there was no mining done adjacent to the southern eighteen miles of track - and from November until April of 1906/07 wind-driven snow blocked tracks for weeks on end. While trains were immobilized, horses and sleighs continued to get through, as they had during the past six winters. The camps on Hunker, Dominion, Quartz, and Sulphur Creeks still had to depend on teamsters to forward goods several miles from the KMR terminal at Sulphur Springs, or directly from Dawson. Instead of profits of several hundred thousands of dollars expected, the railway lost $60,000 in the first nine months of operation.

Lawther and Latta, of course, put off construction of the Stewart River extension, and by October of 1907 decided to shut down operations over the winter months. So it was: Sulphur Springs would remain the southernmost point on the KMR, and the railway would never again operate between the months of October and April. With the introduction of full scale dredging on the creeks of the Klondike after 1908, the railway degenerated from prospects of much high class freight and passenger business to the reality of hauling cordwood to the steam generating plants used for thawing frozen ground ahead of the advancing dredges - and total elimination of passenger service by 1911. A spurt in cordwood hauling activity about this time prompted purchase of KMR engine No. 4, built new for the railway in early 1912 - the first three engines had all served previously with the White Pass and Yukon Route.

The first years of the KMR had seen deficit operation, but in the final three years some miniscule profit was generated. In October of 1913 KMR trains ran for the last time. The KMR was held by Lawther and Latta until 1925 when, in an amalgamation of several Klondike properties, the rolling stock and line of the KMR came under the ownership of the newly-chartered Yukon Consolidated Gold Corporation - Lawther and Latta later served as executives of this new concern.

Chapter 1

Three Creeks with
Three Railways

Origins

Fuel for the burgeoning population of the Klondike was an
absolute necessity, and although the foremost fuel would always
be wood, coal was mined in the district for local use. There
were a number of locations within 100 miles of Dawson City
where beds of coal outcropped, and several companies did
develop mines. Two of the mining companies built railways to
haul the coal to the banks of the Yukon River where steamboats
picked up barge-loads destined for Dawson. These coal mines
were located downstream from Dawson, one on Cliff Creek and
the other on Coal Creek, both tributary creeks of the Yukon
River. The railways serving the coal mines were built and
operated by, respectively, the North American Transportation
and Trading Company (NAT&TCo) and the Coal Creek Coal
Company (CCCCo). The latter company and its railway,
however, were subsequently taken over, in turn, by the
Sourdough Coal Company and the Northern Light, Power and
Coal Company (NLP&CCo.).

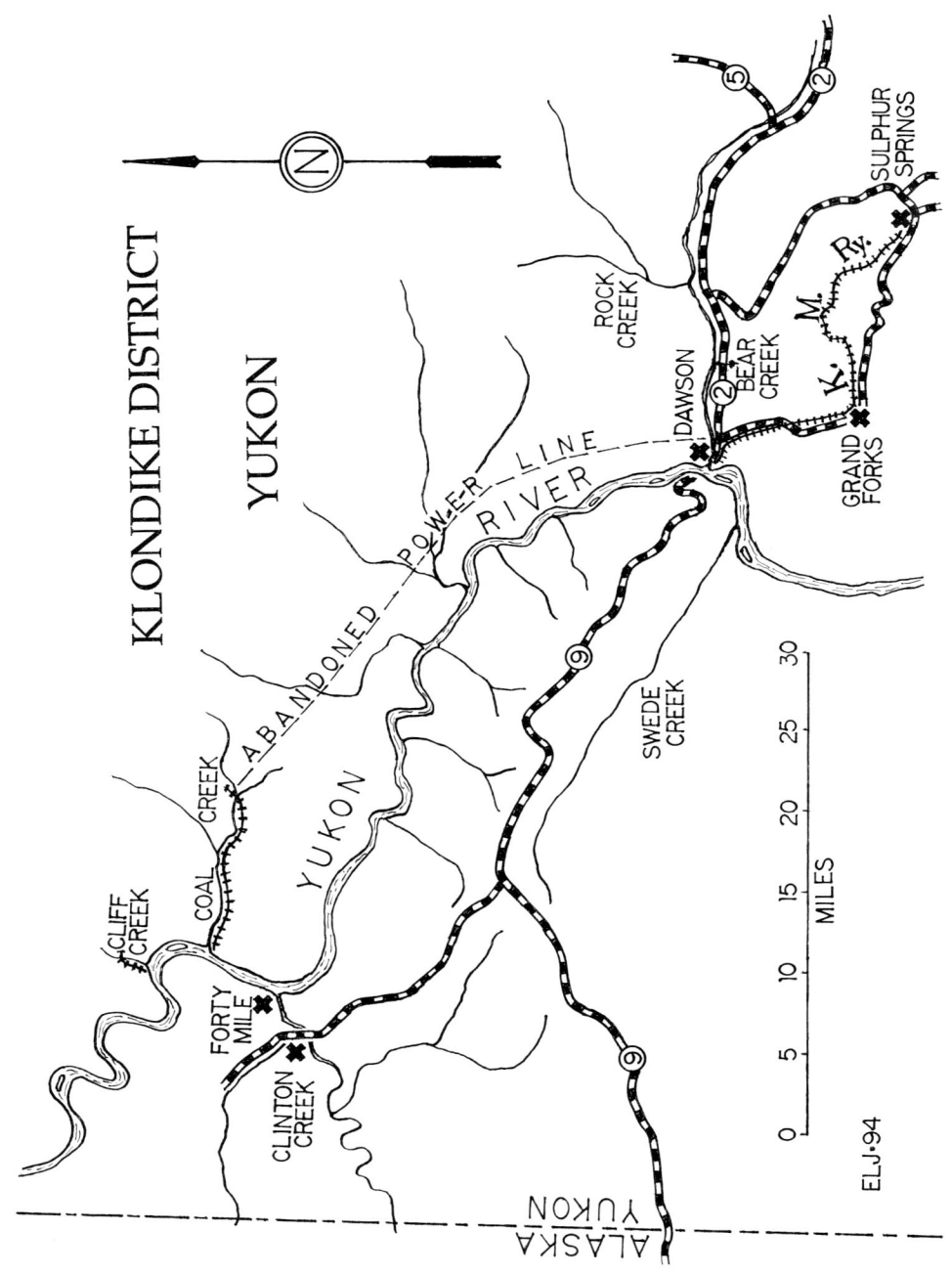

Coal from the Cliff Creek and Coal Creek areas was low-grade lignite, which does not keep well and produces much ash. While coal generally produces about three times the energy from the equivalent weight of spruce wood (one cord of wood weighs about one ton, therefore three cords of wood equal about one ton of coal), coal is not as convenient to handle and store as wood, and additionally burns "dirty and smelly." Steamboat operators experimented with coal for fuel, as did the thawing plants on Bonanza Creek, but both soon returned to cordwood for fuel. However, locomotives of the White Pass and Yukon Route and the Klondike Mines Railway did utilize Yukon coal - for several good reasons coal is preferred over wood in firing locomotives.

Fuel for production of electricity, steam generation, and heating was a major problem in the Klondike. Initially wood provided all the fuel needed. Enormous volumes were cut in the late 1890s and early part of the 1900s, when the population of the Klondike rose to over 30,000. In 1905 more than 15,000 cords of spruce wood were cut. This amount is difficult to compre- hend - one cord of wood is a pile four feet high, by four feet wide, by eight feet long, therefore, 15,000 cords translates to a pile of wood four feet high and four feet wide by twenty-two miles long - and more than 30,000 cords were cut in each of 1900 and 1901! Wood was cut along the Yukon River, up the Stewart and Pelly Rivers, and in the Klondike itself, the hills and valleys were very quickly denuded of trees.

For the better part of the years between 1900 to 1914, the Dawson Electric Light and Power Company (DEL&PCo) relied on local coal to feed the steam-driven turbines, burning wood when the coal supply was intermittently interrupted. The NAT&TCo mine on Cliff Creek produced coal from 1899 until 1903, and the mines on Coal Creek produced coal, rather erratically, from 1903 until about 1915.

3

The third mining railway of the Klondike was short-lived - owned by the Detroit Yukon Mining Company (DYMCo), it was operated on gold placer claims on Bear Creek, six miles up the Klondike River from Dawson. In the early days of the Klondike, gold mining was done with much manual labour - shaft sinking, and mining and stock-piling frozen ground over the winter for washing in spring. As the richest of gravels were worked out, mechanization to handle greater volumes of lower-paying ground came into use: elevators, hydraulicking, drag-lining, and so on. Many operations used very light rail tramways, commonly used in underground mines, where men pushed carloads of pay dirt to sluicing plants - these could not strictly be called railways. At the mouth of Bear Creek, DYMCo brought in two steam shovels, four industrial locomotives, and twenty-four mine cars, and for a short time operated a railway which hauled pay dirt to a sluicing plant on the Klondike River. This railway - as a mining railway - operated for less than one year, although the equipment was put to limited use in other ways for another ten years.

Neither of the coal mine railways nor the railway on Bear Creek were chartered as railways, and therefore should not be referred to as the Bear Creek Railway, the Cliff Creek Railway, or the Coal Creek Railway - they were simply the railway on Bear Creek, or the Detroit Yukon Mining Company's railway on Bear Creek, and so on.

Porter locomotive, engine No. 1, built for the Detroit Yukon Mining Company in 1904, was brought to the Klondike for a mining operation, but was little used except for some construction work for the successor Canadian Klondyke Mining Company. Idle after 1913, the locomotive lay unused at the Bear Creek camp (which was owned by the Yukon Consolidated Gold Corporation after 1925) until 1965, when it was bought by Roger Brammall, and eventually found its way to Vancouver Island. Photo taken in late 1959.

Environment Canada, Parks, courtesy G. Allen Gould, GS 1.2-22

Chapter 2

The Railway on Cliff Creek

The North American Transportation and Trading Company

The Cliff Creek coal mine was owned and operated by the North American Transportation & Trading Company (NAT&TCo) and was in production from 1899 until mid-1903, when coal veins were worked out. Said to be of "superior quality", the coal was classed as lignite. The NAT&TCo was given license to mine in the Yukon Territory on the 17th of May, 1900, for minerals other than coal, since the company's coal mine had already begun shipping in 1899. A 1-3/4 mile, 36-inch gauge, railway ran up Cliff Creek connecting the mine with the shipping terminal on the Yukon River. This terminal was fifty-eight miles downstream from Dawson City, and nine miles downstream from the town of Fortymile, Yukon Territory. Cliff Creek flows down a narrow valley, falling approximately 500 feet or more from the mine to the Yukon River, which translates to a railway grade of 5% or steeper. Although mining at Cliff Creek ceased in 1903, coal had been stock-piled and was shipped until 1904.

The NAT&TCo was known as "Captain Healy's company" and the Cliff Creek mine was referred to as the "Healy mine" - John Healy himself operated out of Dawson at the time. Originally from Fort Benton, Montana, where he had once been sheriff, John J. Healy had in the early 1870s been a trader in the Whoop-Up country north of Montana. Across the border in the Black-foot country of Canada, Healy and his partner, Alfred B. Hamilton, had set up Fort Hamilton in 1869, a notorious "whiskey post" soon to be nick-named "Fort Whoop-Up." With the arrival of North West Mounted Police in 1874, the infamous post was abandoned, Healy and company unwilling to deal lawfully with the Indians. By 1887 Healy had established a trading post at Dyea, Alaska, and by 1892 the route to the Yukon Territory via Dyea and the Chilkoot Pass was in common use. With the backing of Chicago capital, he established the NAT&TCo that year to begin trading on the lower Yukon River; backers included the Corn Exchange Bank of Chicago. The company's operating quarters were at Hamilton near the mouth of the Yukon River, and by 1898 the NAT&TCo had seven sternwheelers freighting between St. Michael, Alaska, and Dawson City, Yukon Territory.

The first official reports, dated August 18, 1896, of William Ogilvie's explorations mention coal veins on Coal Creek, Shell Creek, Twelve Mile Creek, and Cliff Creek; these finds had been made in the 1880s. A subsequent report from Ogilvie, Commis-sioner of the Yukon Territory, on September 20, 1899, added:

> The fuel of Dawson heretofore has been wood, but coal is found in abundance along the Yukon River at various points, and last winter the NAT&TCo opened up and dug out several thousand tons from one of its coal locations which it had acquired, and is now plac-ing coal for sale in Dawson. The same company has imported a considerable number of coal stoves...

7

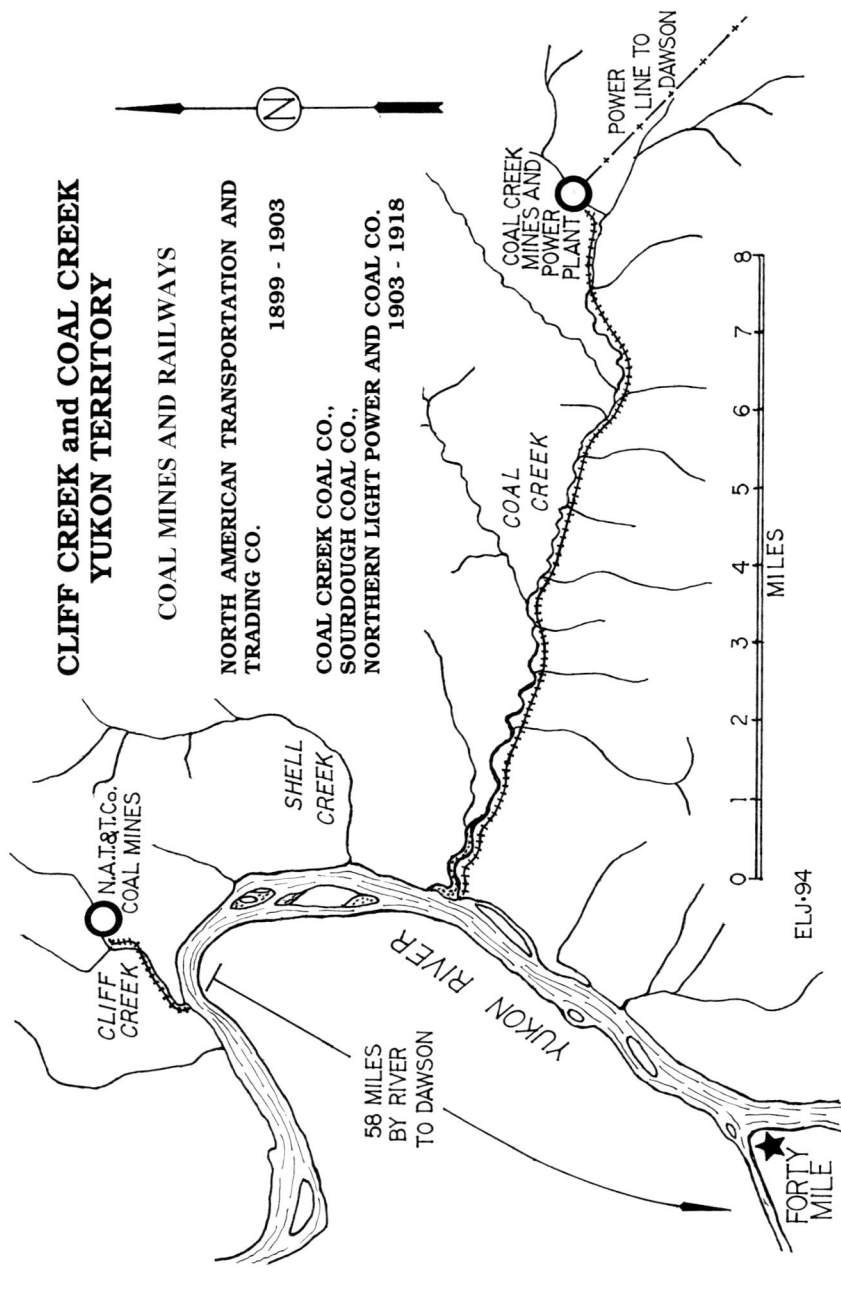

CLIFF CREEK and COAL CREEK
YUKON TERRITORY

COAL MINES AND RAILWAYS

NORTH AMERICAN TRANSPORTATION AND
TRADING CO.   1899 - 1903

COAL CREEK COAL CO.,
SOURDOUGH COAL CO.,
NORTHERN LIGHT POWER AND COAL CO.   1903 - 1918

N.A.T.&T.Co.
COAL MINES

CLIFF CREEK

SHELL CREEK

YUKON RIVER

58 MILES
BY RIVER
TO DAWSON

FORTY MILE

COAL CREEK

COAL CREEK
MINES AND
POWER PLANT

POWER LINE TO DAWSON

MILES

0 1 2 3 4 5 6 7 8

ELJ·94

An editorial in the Dawson Daily News, November 20, 1899, commented;

Coal the Coming Fuel -
The only mine that is yet known to be in production of good results is the Healy mine below Fortymile which, practically is supplying all the coal now used in Dawson.

The mine produced about 4000 tons of coal per year.

In late 1898 the NAT&TCo had begun developing a group of lignite seams 1-3/4 miles up Cliff Creek, and by January of 1899, the company had a force of seventeen men on the property. By mid-summer an incline had been run through a vein of coal for a distance of 400 feet, although the size of the vein was as yet unknown. The railway from the river to the mine was in August still uncompleted because of "the failure of the spikes to arrive from St. Michael with the railroad iron." However, mining was already underway, hauled to riverside load-outs by horse and wagon; on July 26, 1899, the independent steamer *Clara*, pushing the barge *Monarch*, brought the first shipment of Cliff Creek coal to Dawson. NAT&TCo advertisements read,

> Good coal for sale by the
> **North American Transportation**
> **& Trading Company**,
> 1000 tons, can be delivered immediately, apply at office; $30.00/ton.

A Porter saddle-tank locomotive arrived in August or September, and the Dawson Daily News, Midsummer Number, September 1899, read, "The N.A.T.&T.Co. owns and operates the only railroad in the Yukon Territory, in connection with its large coal mining industry."

Built in March, 1899, by the H.K. Porter Company of Pittsburgh, Pennsylvania, the 0-4-0, saddle-tank, 36-inch gauge locomotive, construction number (c/n) 1972, was bought new by the NAT&TCo for the Cliff Creek railway. With boiler pressure of 140 psi, and with 2915 lb of tractive effort, the locomotive had 24-inch wheels, 6x10-inch cylinders, and weighed seven tons empty. Except for having a straight stack and a

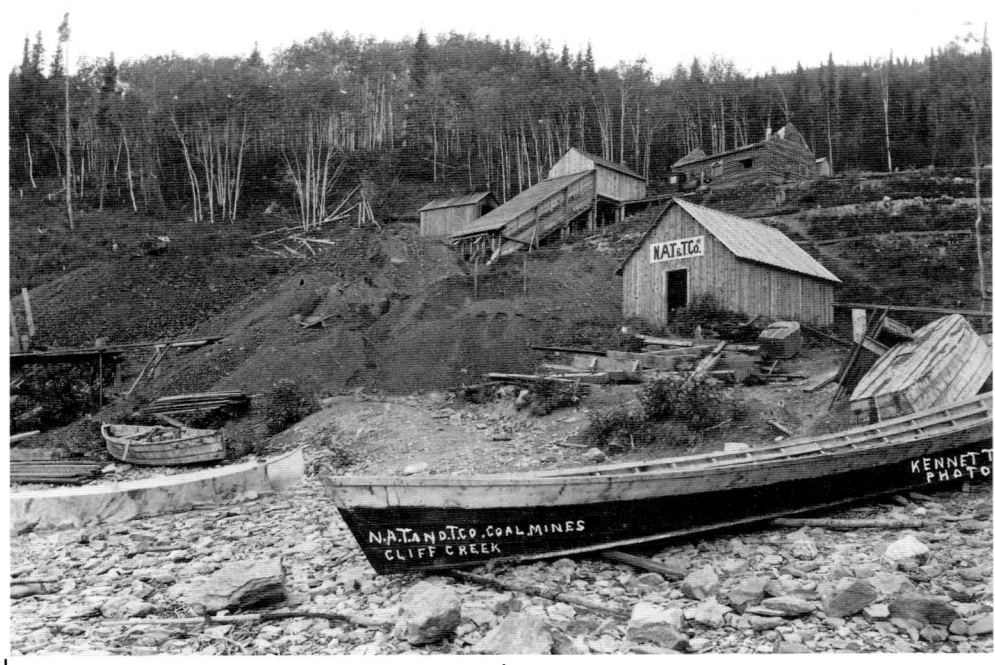

The developer of the coal mine on Cliff Creek was the North American Transportation and Trading Company, and the mine would produce until 1903, when coal reserves were worked out. From the condition of the 7-ton Porter locomotive, visible just above the peak of the NAT&TCo building, this photo was taken in 1899, when the Cliff Creek mine was just being opened up.
Museum of History and Industry Seattle, 9532

longer smoke box, it was very similar to the four Porter locomotives later brought to the Klondike District by the Detroit Yukon Mining Company. The locomotive was equipped with a smokebox number plate, probably No. 1, the cab was lettered N.A.T.&T.Co., and it was without doubt delivered by one of the company's seven steamers early that summer, via St. Michael, Alaska. The company also had brought in at least six short-wheelbase, wooden-hoppered, coal wagons for use on the railway. There were also some 18- or 24-inch gauge mine cars for tramming underground.

With the arrival of KMR engine No. 1 in Klondike City in September of 1902, (thought by some to be the first locomotive in the north), the Yukon Sun informed all that in fact the Cliff Creek engine was the first locomotive to reach the Klondike.

The NAT&TCo continued to advertise in Dawson newspapers, and by late 1902 the company had hired the steamers *Tyrrell* and *J.P. Light* to barge coal to Dawson; the steamers were two of three owned by the Dawson and White Horse Navigation Company (D&WHNCo)[1]. It was thought the Cliff Creek mine might not be able to supply the demand for coal in Dawson. Workings consisted of two long tunnels - the upper 800 feet long - and several drifts and raises

An independent shipping company, the Dawson and White Horse Navigation Company had acquired three steamers in 1900: the *Tyrrell*, the *J.P. Light*, and the *Lightning*, and built three barges: the *Jean*, *Louise*, and *Margaret*. Among the shareholders of the company were "Black" Sullivan, and manager Thomas W. O'Brien, also of the KMR, and owner, or part-owner, of many other business enterprises in the Klondike.

---

1) The charter of the company used the name Dawson White Horse Navigation Company (no *and*) and White Horse as two words, even though the name of the town was Whitehorse.

The shipping company did not survive for long - it was squeezed out by the White Pass on the upper Yukon, and by the big American companies on the lower river. In 1903 the *Lightning* was sold to the Coal Creek Coal Company, but the remaining two steamers worked locally, and for a time freighted coal to Dawson from the mines on Cliff Creek and Coal Creek. By late 1904 both the *Tyrrell* and the *J.P. Light* had been sold.

Three steamboats, the **Tyrrell** *on the right, the* **Lightning** *on the left, and the* **J.P. Light** *behind, were originally operated in 1899 by the British-America Corporation, but in 1900 all were sold to a new concern, the Dawson and White Horse Navigation Company. Three new barges, the* **Jean**, **Margaret**, *and* **Louise**, *were built in anticipation of good business. Seen here at Klondike City, probably about 1901, the three steamers were each built by different shipyards. At one time or another, all three hauled coal, under contract, from the mines on Cliff Creek and Coal Creek, and the* **Lightning** *was in 1903 sold to the Coal Creek Coal Company.*
Yukon Archives, VPL Coll'n, 2162

The steamer **Tyrrell** in the early 1900s. At 678 gross tons, the **Tyrrell** was 142 feet in length by 32 feet in width, built in 1898 at Vancouver, B.C. It was a steel-hulled boat, the only one so equipped on the Yukon River at the time, and of deep draft. Among the owners were the Dawson and White Horse Navigation Company (which did some freighting for the NAT&TCo and the Coal Creek Coal Co), and the British Yukon Navigation Company (the White Pass) which scrapped the steamer at West Dawson in 1912, using the machinery for a new boat.

University of Washington neg. 14803

Under Captain McLean, Tom O'Brien's *Tyrrell* was in collier and excursion service in 1903. With ice still on the upper Yukon River in late May, the *Tyrrell* steamed down to Coal Creek where a new coal development was in progress, then to Cliff Creek. The NAT&TCo had 1000 tons of coal here, sacked and ready for shipment to Dawson, but spring ice had driven the company's barge, brought down last fall, twenty feet above the shore line, where it was perched on large cakes of ice. On the 24th of June the *Tyrrell* again went to Cliff Creek, this time picking up a 75-ton barge-load of coal and delivering it to Eagle, Alaska, for the NAT&TCo.

The steamer *J.P. Light*, which had been inactive since October of 1902, when it was hauling coal from the Cliff Creek mine, was once more fired up on August 10 and, chartered to the NAT&TCo, sailed for St. Michael.

Although the NAT&TCo still had fifteen men at work in mid-June of 1903, coal veins at the Cliff Creek mine were nearly worked out, and in early August the mine was shut down. Over the summer, miners had built up a stock-pile of coal. With no further production the company pulled out all staff except for a watchman at the riverside load-out. The NAT&TCo then sold the locomotive and coal cars to the Coal Creek Coal Company, just now developing its property up-river. (It was fortunate for the NAT&TCo that another mining railway was starting up just as they wanted to get rid of their rolling stock.) In the first week of August the steamer *S.S. Bailey*, on a return trip from Eagle, was hired to freight Porter locomotive c/n 1972 and the rest of the rolling stock from Cliff Creek to the Coal Creek landing. The Cliff Creek engine would go to work alongside two, "new," bigger, 0-6-0 Porters locomotives.

14

Late in its short career on the NAT&TCo's Cliff Creek railway is the Porter locomotive. The well-used look of the track indicates this was about 1902 or 1903. Coal mined here was a rather low-quality lignite. The locomotive and cars were shipped to the mine on Coal Creek in 1903.

British Columbia Archives and Records Service, 76827

At Cliff Creek in 1903, the NAT&TCo still had coal to ship, and the company hired Tom O'Brien's steamers, the *Tyrrell* and the *J.P. Light*, to deliver its stock-piled coal. In October, with the navigation season about to close, the company had 700 to 800 tons in Dawson, and 1000 tons still at the mine. In June of 1904 the *J.P. Light* brought the last of the company's coal to Dawson, to end the life of the Cliff Creek coal mine.

With business on the decline in the Klondike, the NAT&TCo sold its fleet of steamers to the Merchants Yukon Transportation Company in 1906, and in 1912 sold its mercantile business to the Northern Commercial Company.

The last word about the NAT&TCo mine was on July 25, 1918, when the Dawson Daily News reported; "two miles of railroad track at the old Cliff Creek mine are being torn up, for sale to the outside by purchaser Mr. Kemp."

The steamer **J.P. Light**, shoving a barge, has stopped somewhere on the Yukon River in Alaska to replenish its wood supply. The **J.P. Light** was, at 785 tons gross, 176 feet in length and 35 feet in width. It was built at Seattle in 1898 by the Moran Brothers and was one of twelve (including the **Mary F. Graff**) that steamed north for gold rush business on the Yukon River - the maze of truss cables and hog posts make for quick identification of the Moran steamers. The **J.P. Light** was contracted to haul coal from the Cliff Creek mine and, for a short time, from the mines on Coal Creek. Like its partners the **Tyrrell** and the **Lightning**, it would also end service with the White Pass, and was abandoned at St. Michael, Alaska, in 1927.

University of Washington, neg. 7817

Chapter 3

The Railway on Coal Creek
Part I

Overview

Built by the Coal Creek Coal Company (CCCCo), a substantial 36-inch gauge railway operated on Coal Creek, a stream which joins the Yukon River from the east, four miles above Cliff Creek and 54 miles below Dawson. In contrast to Cliff Creek, Coal Creek meanders down a broad valley bottom, falling only 500 feet in the twelve miles from mines to the Yukon River. Rail grades in general did not exceed 1%, but the line crossed dozens of streams which had to be bridged, many subject to washouts by spring floods. Coal mining on the south fork of Coal Creek started in 1903, although full scale shipments did not begin until 1904. The property was operated as the Sourdough Coal Company from late 1906 until 1909 when it was sold to the Northern Light, Power, and Coal Company (NLP&CCo). This company acquired the railway and two locomotives, bought a Shay locomotive, and built a thermal-electric plant near the mine, but after a few years of intermittent operation the power plant was shut down permanently in 1914. Coal may have been

Taken about mid-August of 1903, this photo shows construction of the last mile on the Coal Creek Coal Company's railway. On spruce ties, slabbed on two side only and sawn by a company-owned sawmill halfway up the line, light weight rail of 36-inch gauge is being laid. Built so close to Coal Creek, and crossing numerous feeder streams, the railway was subject to washouts every spring.
Yukon Archives, Dawson City Museum Collection, 6338

mined in 1915, and it appears the railway may have been used as late as 1918 when salvagers hauled power plant equipment down to the Yukon River landing.

There was another Coal Creek in the Klondike on which coal was also mined, but this mine did not have a railway. The Rock Creek Coal Mine, owned by the Alaska Exploration Company,

was started up in July of 1899. This mine was situated on Coal
Creek, a tributary of Rock Creek, seven miles up from the
Klondike River, and twenty miles east from Dawson. A wagon
road led from Dawson to the mine. The Rock Creek mine was
short-lived, probably because of the problem of transportation to
Dawson. The property was re-examined in 1937 and 1938 after
a wood shortage had developed in the district, but the mine was
not put into production.

About 150 miles down-river from the village of Fortymile, there
was a third, better-known, Coal Creek. Well within the State of
Alaska, this Coal Creek - also a feeder of the Yukon River - was
the site of a long-lived and profitable gold-dredging operation.

The Coal Creek Coal Company

Coal was discovered on Coal Creek and other locations in the
Fortymile area during the 1880s, and at the time of the discovery
of gold on Bonanza Creek in 1896, Henry Siemer had already
laid claim to some properties on Coal Creek. About 1902 James
Williams became interested in the holdings. On January 20,
1903, the Canada Gazette announced that the Coal Creek Coal
Company had been issued a letters patent dated January 12,
1903. Incorporated under patent, the syndicate included: Falcon
Joslin, broker; James Anderson Williams, capitalist; Henry
Siemer, miner; August Carlson, miner; all of Dawson in the
Yukon Territory; and Carl Magnus Johanson, commissioner, of
Circle City, District of Alaska. Falcon Joslin, chief promoter,
advertised his services in early Dawson newspapers;

Falcon Joslin
broker; conveyances, rents, real estate, loans and
collections, reports on mines and mining properties -
investment properties, insurance, annuities...

19

He had arrived in Dawson in 1897, one of the first lawyers here, and was instrumental in formation of the Dawson Electric Light and Power Company, of which he was secretary. That company had been organized with $75,000 in capital, with Billy Chappell president and Alex MacDonald vice-president.

Williams and Siemer had begun developing the Coal Creek property in 1902 and by January 28, 1903, John Joslin - brother of Falcon - reported that a shaft inclined at sixty-five degrees had been sunk for 250 feet to the coal vein, where the workings leveled off. Mine cars running on steel rails were pushed to the base of the incline where a steam-operated hoist hauled them up the incline to a tipple on the surface. The bed of coal varied from four and one-half to eleven feet in thickness; coal mined during this development work was winched to surface and hauled by teams and sleds to bunkers located on the Yukon River. A complete railway "outfit" had already been ordered, with rail for thirteen miles of track.

By mid-April of 1903, a sawmill had been installed halfway up the creek, and men were busy surveying the route, cutting ties, and preparing to build a number of bridges and two coal bunkers - one of 500 tons capacity at the docks on the Yukon River, and one of 250 tons at the mine. By June, 100 men were at work grading the route, although no rails had arrived yet; two engines were on the way.

There was a wood shortage developing in Dawson, and a market for coal was growing. With hopes of the KMR being completed soon, a market was also seen here. There was also a possibility of the many steamers on the river converting from wood to coal for fuel. Although the Cliff Creek coal mine was at this time just being worked out, the mines at Tantalus Bluffs were just being re-opened. Near Carmacks, 225 miles upstream from

Dawson and right on the banks of the Yukon River, coal had been discovered in the 1890s, and after several under-financed attempts to mine, production stopped. Coal from the Tantalus mine, also known as Captain Miller's Mine and later controlled by the Five Finger Coal Company, was classed as semi-bituminous, and of slightly better quality than the lignite of the Cliff Creek and Coal Creek deposits. In early summer the *Tyrrell* brought a barge-load of Tantalus coal to Dawson for testing - this was competition the CCCCo neither expected nor wanted.

In mid-July the grade and bridges of the Coal Creek railway line were ready, and on the 26th, the steamer *Victorian* brought in 275 tons of material, including rails.

On August 4, 1903, the steamer *S.S. Bailey* brought the rolling stock - a 0-4-0 locomotive, six coal cars, and probably some mine cars - from the Cliff Creek railway to the Coal Creek landing. The *S.S. Bailey* had continued on to Whitehorse, where it picked up another load of rail for Coal Creek. About August 6, the steamer *Mary F. Graff* dropped off 240 tons of material, including two larger locomotives, several cars, and rails, at Coal Creek. These locomotives were well-used 0-6-0 saddle-tankers built by the H.K. Porter Company, and from certain features such as the sand domes it is believed they were built before 1890; neither construction numbers, construction dates, nor previous owners of the locomotives are known. One locomotive weighing about twelve tons had 25-inch wheels and 6x12-inch cylinders, the other of about fourteen tons had 27-inch wheels and 8x14-inch cylinders. Road numbers and lettering were not applied to the locomotives, which arrived without smokebox number plates. The haul at Coal Creek was much longer than at the Cliff Creek mine and would have required these substantially bigger engines. In total, twelve cars, in addition to the ex-Cliff Creek rolling stock, were also delivered to Coal Creek - some

21

short flats and some coal wagons. By this time, five of 11-1/2 miles of railway track had been built and the company had three locomotives and more than twelve cars on the property. In early September, the Coal Creek railway was completed, and president J.A. Williams drove the last spike.

The date - August 3, 1903, the place - the White Pass docks at Dawson. Just arrived on the Moran-built **Mary F. Graff** are two 0-6-0 Porter locomotives bought by the Coal Creek Coal Company for use on its railway. The unmarked engines appear well-used, probably built prior to 1890. The larger, 14-ton, locomotive on the left has no lamp; the sand dome has been removed from the smaller, 12-ton, locomotive and its lamp has been knocked askew. Neither have handrails. The **Mary F. Graff** would continue on downstream on the Yukon River for 54 miles to Coal Creek, where the engines were unloaded.

National Archives of Canada, PA 16593

The smaller of the two 0-6-0 Porter locomotives brought to Coal Creek in August of 1903. This photo was probably taken in 1903 as construction on the line was being completed.
Yukon Archives, Dawson City Museum Coll'n, 6337

The company now had a 500-ton capacity coal bunker completed in Dawson, and was building a 2000-foot, inclined, narrow-gauge tramway from deep water on the Yukon River to the power house in South Dawson, utilizing rail that was left over from the Coal Creek line. The Dawson Electric Light and Power Company (DEL&PCo) had a thermal generating plant here in Dawson, capable of burning both coal and wood, providing the area with electricity. On the tramway, cars would be pulled by a cable (powered by a hay-burner, as we shall see) from barges to the power house. The coal sold in Dawson for $16/ton; at the time spruce wood sold for $7 to $8/cord in Dawson and $8 to $15 on the creeks - in production of energy, three cords of wood are approximately equal to a ton of coal.

On September 14, 1903, the steamer *Lightning* and the barge *Margaret* (both of which had just been bought by the CCCCo from the D&WHNCo) brought the first load of Coal Creek coal to Dawson. However, this coal was not brought from the mines to the river by the company's railway; it had been stock-piled at the riverside load-out earlier by horse-drawn sled and wagon. While being used to unload the barge, the newly-built tramway at Dawson immediately proved to be less-than-perfect; the horse pulling a 3-ton car up the rail grade from the beach began to be pulled backwards, the horse took off in the same direction, and the car went off the tracks into rocks at the barge.

In late September the railway on Coal Creek was only just being ballasted, when the road bed was damaged by heavy rains, and an engine went over on its side, severely burning the engineer. John Cochrane was badly scalded; he was brought to Fortymile, then to hospital in Dawson. In addition to the engine still laying on its side, two other engines were operating - one at the river, one at the mine.

"The Str. *Lightning* of the D.&W.H. Line Making Record Run Dawson to White Horse on Yukon River, 8 July 1900." *At 557 gross tons the* **Lightning** *was 140 feet in length by 30 feet in width and was built at Vancouver, B.C. in 1898. The Dawson and White Horse Navigation Company sold the* **Lightning** *and the barge* **Margaret** *to the Coal Creek Coal Company in 1903 for use hauling coal to Dawson, and the steamer and barge were passed on to the successor companies, the Sourdough Coal Company in 1906, and the Northern Light, Power and Coal Company in 1909. By 1917, when the* **Lightning** *was scrapped at Dawson, it was the property of the White Pass.*

National Archives of Canada
PA 16228

25

In mid-October Falcon Joslin pulled out all production crews from the Coal Creek mine and shut down the railway. However, a small crew of miners would work through the winter developing new workings for production at start-up next spring.
In the spring of 1904, the *Lightning* (owned by the CCCCo) was out of service, having been driven aground - high above the river level at Fortymile - by ice floes during spring breakup. In

Probably taken in 1903, this photo show the smaller of the pair of 0-6-0 Porter locomotives owned by the Coal Creek Coal Company. On a four-axle flat car, about twenty feet in length, are lengths of light-weight rail.

Eric L. Johnson Collection

June, O'Brien's *J.P. Light*, working as a collier in the hire of
the CCCCo, was dumping coal directly at the wharf of the
DEL&PCo on Fifth Avenue. Moored on the Klondike River, the
J.P. Light was unloaded by wheelbarrows, a slow business; the
inclined tramway built only last September had apparently been
found unsafe and unworkable.

O'Brien's other steamer, the *Tyrrell*, was in excursion service up
the Yukon River (- good music - round trip - $1.00); the J.P.
Light was chartered by the CCCCo for a trip to Coal Creek
where manager Williams toured a group of prominent Dawson
businessmen over the railway on a special train.

> One of the big coal cars was fitted up as a passenger
> coach - the side and top were covered with a tarpaulin
> to protect the passengers from rain and cinders. The
> train made good speed through virgin forest. The un-
> derground mine is in full operation, and about 60 men
> are working. The vein is well opened up after several
> years of development, and is capable of great produc-
> tion.

The *J.P. Light* brought back a small cargo of 60 tons of coal.

A month later the *Lightning* was back afloat and the CCCCo
was making arrangements to ship 10,000 tons of coal before the
close of navigation. Much of the coal would go to the
DEL&PCo, "the shareholders of the two companies being much
the same." During the summer of 1904, however, the White
Pass had done exhaustive tests of coal from mines of the Yukon
Territory, and found coal from the Five Finger Coal Company to
be superior, subsequently awarding a contract to that company.
Falcon Joslin, chief promoter of the Coal Creek Coal Company,
also promoted and got a charter for the Tanana Mines Railroad
in 1903 (early on, referred to as the "Joslin railroad", and in
1907 renamed the Tanana Valley Railroad). On March 17, 1905,

Joslin left Dawson by team for the Tanana. He reportedly had 180 tons of rail here, and 800 tons more at the mouth of the Hootalinqua, held over since last fall. "Also with this will go a small locomotive which has been purchased from the Coal Creek Coal Company and which is now at that company's wharf." In June of 1905 the steamer *Louise* stopped at Coal Creek and picked up the Porter locomotive (c/n 1972), taking it to Chena for Joslin's Tanana Mines Railroad.

About 1905 or soon after, this photo shows the ex-Cliff Creek, ex-Coal Creek, Porter locomotive c/n 1972 in passenger service on the Tanana Mines Railroad. The locomotive survives today, and is being restored at Fairbanks by the Friends of the Tanana Valley Railroad, Inc.
Univ. of Alaska Archives, Fairbanks, Bunnell, 63-46-293

Arriving at Chena, on the Tanana River in Alaska, the ex-Cliff Creek, ex-Coal Creek, Porter went to work in July, and it would be in service here until 1930, when it was retired. Very fortunately it was not scrapped. After spending many years on display in Fairbanks, "Tanana Valley (Mines) No. 1" is now being restored by the "Friends of the Tanana Valley Railroad, Inc."

An August, 1905, newspaper item reported;

> A load of coal from a new Yukon coal mine arrived at Dawson on a barge with the steamer Victorian. The coal was to be used at the fire hall. The coal came from the Sourdough mine, eight miles below Fortymile, owned by Siemer and Cameron.

Siemer was one of the charter members of the CCCCo, and the Sourdough coal land adjoined the Coal Creek property, right on the rail line.

June of 1906 found J.A. Williams announcing the CCCCo had repaired railway bridges which had been washed out during the spring flood - "more coal will be mined this summer than ever." Although coal bunkers at Klondike City were being filled with Tantalus coal for use on the Klondike Mines Railway, the CCCCo, which was under lease to Williams, was delivering a large tonnage to Dawson for use by the DEL&PCo, most apparently shipped from the Sourdough mine.

Chapter 4

The Railway on Coal Creek
Part II

The Sourdough Coal Company

In late September, 1906, N.A. Fuller, who was president of the Yukon Telephone Syndicate, took over management of the DEL&PCo. He and a partner, Dr. A.S. Grant, then began dealing for property with several enterprises in mind. They had earlier acquired the Grotschier Concession (placer gold) located on the plateau behind Klondike City, and announced that a dredge would be placed on the property.

In early October of 1906, the Yukon World headlined, "Local Capital Now Vies with That of Guggenheims in Large Enterprises." In the past sixty days Fuller and Grant had spent $300,000 in acquisitions: the DEL&PCo light plant, full control of the Grotschier Concession, six square miles of a timber berth, the steamer *Lightning* and two barges, the Sourdough property of 900 acres, the controlling interest in the Coal Creek property of 450 acres, and the twelve-mile Coal Creek railway. Fuller and Grant would operate the coal mines and railway under the

name of the Sourdough Coal Company, a private company
without an official charter.

A grandiose plan for the next twelve months included expen-
diture of $500,000 in construction of a 3000-horsepower
generating plant at the mouth of Coal Creek, with transmission
lines to Dawson. Power would be sold cheaply for all forms of
local use, and additionally would be sold to dredging operations
at Fortymile and in the Klondike District - and on the syndicate's
own Grotschier Concession. The company was also going after
bigger coal sales, and would build a 10,000 ton bunker in
Dawson, so constructed at the river's edge to be able to load
both railway cars and river steamers. Coal was mined full-scale
during 1907, and bunkers were built in Dawson City, but neither
was a power plant built, nor was a dredge installed on the
Grotschier Concession.

In late summer of 1908, the DEL&PCo let a contract for 4000
cords of wood for winter power - that year the mines on Coal
Creek met with difficulties, veins were being worked out and
flooding. A new vein of excellent coal was found, but too late
for Dawson's winter supply. In 1909 the syndicate sold its
Sourdough/Coal Creek interests to the Northern Light, Power
and Coal Company. This company was promoted by E.H.
Thruston of England and was granted operating rights in the
Yukon Territory by the Parliament of Canada .

The Northern Light, Power and Coal Company

Dated May 21, 1909, a letters patent was issued to the Northern
Light, Power and Coal Company, Limited (NLP&CCo) with a
capital stock of three million dollars, allowing the company to
operate in Canada, with the chief place of business in Dawson,

Yukon Territory. It was incorporated under the name of Edmund Heathcote Thruston, Esquire, of London, England, and the applicant list included barristers Andrew Haydon and Wilfred Cheevers Grieg (both junior partners of the omnipresent Harold Buchanan McGiverin, and also executives of the KMR), real estate agent Francis Laderoute, and law clerk Eugene Clancy, all of Ottawa. Fifteen sub-sections listed a wide range of enterprises allowed under the charter, including electricity generation and sale, water works, mining and minerals, timber, navigation, and the purchase of other companies.

The company acquired the Dawson utilities - DEL&PCo, Dawson City Water and Power, and the Yukon Telephone Syndicate, valued at, respectively, $150,000, $50,000, and $65,000 - plus the Coal Creek coal mines and railway, including the steamer *Lightning*, which was valued at $40,000. Near the mines, on the south fork of Coal Creek (about 35 miles north-west of Dawson), NLP&CCo would build a thermal generating plant, intending to sell electricity to Dawson and the dredging companies mining in the Klondike. Through its subsidiary, the DEL&PCo, the NLP&CCo also ordered a new two-truck, Lima Shay, and a pair of flat cars from the White Pass & Yukon Route. With the Coal Creek railway, the NLP&CCo also acquired the two CCCCo Porters and coal cars.

In May of 1909 the NLP&CCo announced that the Coal Creek coal mine, which was closed all of last year, would re-open; thirty to forty miners had already gone to work three weeks ago.

> Dawson Electric Light & Power who own the mine
> used wood all last winter. The company's steamer the
> 'Lightning' which had also been unused for a year had
> settled in the mud below Yukon Sawmills at Klondike
> City, and is now being refurbished to tow barges.
> Captain William Cowley will command.

The June 12, 1909, issue of the Economist listed an issue of $2,000,000 in bonds as first mortgage on the company shown here as "Northern Light and Power Company." A statement claimed $84,500 in profits generated in 1908 by the three Dawson utility companies. The bond issue would be used to

> ...build an electrical power plant to supply Klondike White Channel Gravel Mining Company for not less than ten years.

> This mining company has contracted to take for ten years, 14,000,000 kilowatt hours per annum, of

The date of this photo is unknown - it might be anywhere between 1903 and 1913. The smaller of the two Coal Creek 0-6-0s has stopped to top up its saddle tank - note the lamp on the rear of the locomotive. The occasion is also unknown; there are at least ten men in the picture, and the tarped 20-foot, four-axle, flat car is loaded with lumber and other supplies east-bound to the mines.
Yukon Archives, Marsh Coll'n, 84/85

electric current at a price which is said to show a
profit of over 61,000 English pounds. The fulfillment
of the contract is guaranteed by two gentleman, Mr.
Fuller and Mr. Treadwell, interested in the property.

The Economist cautioned investors; "The venture...is clearly
speculation, but the share bonus may prove valuable."

All through the summer 150 men were at work, at the Coal
Creek mine and in rebuilding the railway. In late August, E.H.
Thruston of the NLP&CCo informed reporters;

> ...the company has bought all the utilities plus the
> properties of the associated coal company, including
> the claims on Coal Creek, the railway, the steamer
> Lightning and wharves, buildings and bunkers. The
> railroad has been overhauled. The company will be
> building a 6000 kW, coal-fired, power station.
> Electricity will be delivered to Dawson by a forty mile
> power line to be strung. Coal will also be delivered
> for sale to Dawson. Financed by English capital, the
> company has 2,500 tons of equipment now in
> shipment across the ocean. At the mine 4-1/2 million
> tons of coal have been blocked out.

On August 26, 1909, a Shay locomotive arrived at Klondike
City for the Coal Creek railway. The Dawson Daily News in
early September wrote;

> A locomotive with shay gearing has been assembled
> the last few days at the roundhouse of the Klondike
> Mines Railway for use on the Northern Light, Power
> and Coal Company's line. The first of its type in the
> Yukon, it was built to order in Ohio, and is designed
> for hauling heavy long trains. Power is applied to the
> wheels of the tender as well as the locomotive. The

engine is a wood burner, not designed for speed. The
engine was sent knocked down and assembled here
without plan or instructions, which have been delayed
somewhere along the route. [It was] needed to handle
the additional traffic at the property.

The report erred on one point - a wood-burner at a coal mine?
The September 21, 1909, Dawson News quoted Mr. Thruston,
saying, "Our shay locomotive is a big success and is hauling
loads over the tracks with ease."

The Shay was built in July of 1909 by the Lima Locomotive
Works of Lima, Ohio, c/n 2190; records indicate it was sold to
the Dawson Electric Light and Power Company, a subsidiary of
the NLP&CCo, and may have been lettered so. Of 36-inch
gauge, the two-truck locomotive weighed 24 tons (48,416 lb),
had 10,677 lb of tractive effort, 26½-inch wheels, and two
8x12-inch cylinders; the locomotive carried 830 gallons of water
and one ton of coal. Arriving with the locomotive were two
flatcars, refurbished and sold by the White Pass & Yukon
Route, to the DEL&PCo.

Coal mining continued with 140 tons a day being landed at the
Coal Creek bunkers, while other crews laid out a power line
right-of-way and distributed the power poles for the line leading
to the Dawson area - although the line would not be strung until
next year. On October 28, 1909, the equipment for the thermal
plant was unloaded from the ocean steamer *Lonsdale* in
Vancouver, but it not freighted north until the next spring.

By June of 1910 equipment began arriving at Coal Creek -
including cement for generator and turbine bases - and part of
the plant was in place and operating by September. Six 2000-
horsepower boilers were delivered, but only four installed; of

seven generators on the property, capable of producing 9000 kW, only enough for 2500 kW were installed. Electric power from this plant was used only by dredges on Bonanza Creek and the Klondike River. Coal was shipped from the mine to Dawson City and stock-piled at the DEL&PCo thermal plant to provide power for domestic use during the coming year, and for sale locally. In early winter the company had nearly 60 men at work at Coal Creek, but when the dredges shut down on December 20, the power house at Coal Creek was also shut down; about 25 men stayed on to mine coal through the winter. In that year

In the summer of 1910, the Northern Light, Power, and Coal Company was in the midst of construction of its thermal-electric plant near the coal mines on the south fork of Coal Creek. Coal mines are on both sides of the valley, at mid-ground is the power house, transformer house, and tipple, and uphill at the upper right is the power line right-of-way, leading to Dawson some 40 miles away. The eastern terminus of the railway, which ran along the valley bottom, was here at the mines.

Yukon Archives, Forrest Coll'n, 80/60 153

about 10,000 tons of coal were mined. In 1911 the power plant operated only from May until June but did not operate at all during 1912. 10,000 tons of coal were mined in 1911, and 6500 tons in 1912.

Coal from the Coal Creek mine fired the company-owned DEL&PCo thermal-electric plant in Dawson City for local sale of power, and initially the new plant on Coal Creek sold power to the dredging companies. But the demand from the latter was irregular, and with the completion of hydroelectric plants built by the Granville Power Company (Yukon Gold Company) in 1910 and 1911, the Coal Creek plant could not compete and was shut down. The NLP&CCo still mined coal however, and had the steamer *Lightning* still in service. An ad of August 1912 assured Dawsonites that there would be 6000 tons of coal in the company's bunkers in Dawson before winter, for local sale.

NLP&CCo had hoped to gain contracts with the other coal consumers in the Yukon, but up-river the Five Finger Coal Company (incorporated in the State of Minnesota) had in 1909 obtained control of the Tantalus and Tantalus Butte properties to create formidable competition. The Five Finger Coal Company had signed contracts with the White Pass, the KMR, and the Yukon Gold Company. Not only was Five Finger coal of better quality, the mines were right at river's edge, and therefore coal was deliverable at a lower cost. (The two Tantalus properties were situated on either side of the Yukon River about ten miles below Five Finger Rapids, while the Five Finger mine was about sixteen miles below Tantalus - or eight miles as the crow flies.) In mid-August of 1912 the Five Finger Coal Company advertised, simply,

Tantalus Coal - the Coal of Quality and Economy.

Oops! DYMCo Porter No. 3 has gone off the end of track at the Coal Creek loadout on the Yukon River, 1913 or 1914. It was successfully yarded out.
Yukon Archives, Marsh Coll'n, 84/85

The NLP&CCo countered with a somewhat desperate response,

Coal Creek Coal...cheap, high-class, clean...coal now being mined is almost the difference between lignite and bituminous...support Dawson industries, we are big employers of labour, this helps you.

In mid-February, 1913, Joe Boyle of the Canadian Klondyke Mining Company leased the plant and operation of the NLP&CCo. Power was needed to drive two new dredges now working in the valley of the Klondike River. On June 23, 1913, the Dawson Daily News reported;

The plant of the NLP&CCo at Coal Creek is being put
into condition for service. Manager J.W. Boyle
started work last week. The steam-electric plant will
be overhauled for use in case of emergency - if the
North Fork hydroelectric plant might shut down
temporarily. The railroad track from the coal mine
and powerhouse to the Yukon River is being
improved. A dummy engine and small cars, which
were used for excavating for the Canadian Klondike
Mining Company dredges, were sent to Coal Creek to
displace the larger and heavier cars on the line. They
left on the Lightning Saturday; Captain Billy Cowley
is master of the Lightning again this season.

The dummy engine referred to was a Porter 0-4-0 saddle-tanker,
No. 3, one of four brought to the Yukon for the Detroit Yukon
Mining Company in 1904. That summer advertisements read;

> Coal $7.75/ton, Northern Light Coal,
> Joseph W. Boyle.

Coal Creek coal was not the choice of industry, however; an
advertisement placed in newspapers during 1913 by the Five
Finger Coal Company read;

> Tantalus coal used exclusively by the railways of the
> Yukon Territory and large fuel consumers.

- i.e. both the White Pass & Yukon Route and the KMR.

In March of 1913 a gold mine near Juneau, Alaska, was being
readied for production. The Alaska-Gastineau Mining Company
began work on two hydroelectric dams on nearby Salmon Creek
that spring, and it was announced that, "the wooden tramway

which now runs up the canyon is to be relaid with steel rails and locomotive substituted for horses." An 8-ton Porter went to work at the lower dam in May, and on June 3, 1913, the NLP&CCo Shay arrived for duty hauling supplies on the steeper upper section of the tram road. Exactly when the Shay left Coal Creek isn't known, but it did leave in the fall of 1912 or earlier, since shipping on the Yukon River does not usually open until

The time is 10:00 p.m. on June 19 of 1913, and there is lots of daylight available on the longest day of the year, in the Land of the Midnight Sun. Joe Boyle of the Canadian Klondyke Mining Co. had just leased the entire plant of the NLP&CCo on Coal Creek, and was shipping this under-utilized locomotive for service there. Note the massive freight wagon pulled by six horses - the locomotive is small but weighed seven tons. It was taken by wagon from the dredge site to the docks, then by steamer **Lightning** to Coal Creek. DYMCo No. 3 was not much used at Coal Creek, and was abandoned there in 1918.
Vancouver Public Library, 16961

the first week of June. The Salmon Creek dam was complete by late 1914, and it seems likely that the Shay remained here until the sale of all Alaska-Gastineau property about 1920.

In July of 1914, an NLP&CCo bondholder, Oscar Newhouse, launched a case against the NLP&CCo and subsidiary companies, J.W. Boyle and trustees, and the bondholders of the parent company, disputing the legality of the lease signed by Joe Boyle (of the Canadian Klondyke Mining Company - CKMCo). On the 29th, courts declared the lease null and void. The defendants were listed as: Yukon Telephone Syndicate, Ltd., Dawson City Water and Power Company, Ltd., Dawson Electric Light and Power Company, Ltd., Yukon Exploration Limited, Joseph Whiteside Boyle, Harold Buchanan McGiverin, Napoleon Antoine Belcourt, and the trustees for the NLP&CCo. Meanwhile, Boyle had solved problems with his hydroelectric plants, and now had no further need for the NLP&CCo plant anyway.

It is believed the Coal Creek mines were worked in 1914 and possibly into 1915 to supply fuel for the DEL&PCo plant. Records indicate both CKMCo and the Yukon Gold Company were interested in the power plant but no deals were made. By 1916 several bridges on the Coal Creek railway were knocked out during spring floods, and it seems doubtful if there was any activity on Coal Creek during that year.

In September of 1917 crews landed at Coal Creek and, at the head of the railway, began the job of dismantling the power plant, which had not been operated for four years, for shipment to the outside. Through the winter men worked, knocking apart buildings to make packing crates, and by the time the shipping season opened in June of 1918, several thousand tons of freight were waiting at the riverside landing. Whether the salvagers had rebuilt the rail line or used horse and sled for haulage is not

Lima Shay c/n 2190 was bought new in 1909 for use in construction of the Northern Light, Power, and Coal Company's coal-fired power plant on Coal Creek. Exactly when it left Coal Creek isn't known, but in early June of 1913 it arrived at Juneau and went to work in construction of Alaska-Gastineau's hydro dam on nearby Salmon Creek - pictured here about that time. The Shay eventually reached the Biles-Coleman Lumber Company at Omak, Washington, and its life was ended there - scrapped about 1940.

Alaska State Library, Juneau, Gastonguay Coll'n, PCA 119-162

known, but the three (or four?) locomotives were parked at the Yukon River terminal where several flat cars and mine cars were also abandoned. The June 13, 1918, issue of the Dawson Daily News stated that the NLP&CCo plant at Coal Creek had been dismantled, the equipment going to Japan, Canada, and the United States - shipped via St. Michael. The last act was the taking up of the rails as the last cars moved out. Although the Shay had been shipped out years earlier, the three Porter locomotives were abandoned here, apparently not worth their weight in scrap iron.

The NLP&CCo had been organized largely as a speculative scheme with little chance of success. More than $2 million had been spent on the project, and legal actions against the former owners of the properties continued over the years as bond-holders fought to gain control of the company. The Dawson utilities, subsidiaries of the NLP&CCo, were operated by a succession of dredging companies until taken over by the YCGC in 1925. The utilities were operated with little or no profit until 1966 when the YCGC's last dredges were shut down, and at that time the shares of the utility companies were sold to an agency of the federal government. The original bond- and share-holders received nothing.

The first locomotive on the Coal Creek railway was the ex-Cliff Creek locomotive, c/n 1972, which arrived on about August 4, 1903. It worked here until sold to the Tanana Mines Railroad in March of 1905, leaving Coal Creek in June. The little Porter went to work on the Tanana Mines (Valley) Railroad, which subsequently became part of the Alaska Railroad, staying here until 1930 when it was put on display in Fairbanks. Here it deteriorated, vandalized, until recent times when the Friends of the Tanana Valley Railroad, Inc. got control of the locomotive; today it is undergoing complete restoration by a dedicated group of rail fans, and it may once again become operable.

The NLP&CCo Shay, which left Coal Creek in 1912, and arrived at Juneau in 1913, probably remained on the Salmon Creek tramway until the mine was shut down. The Alaska-Gastineau gold mine was shut down in 1920 when "operations became unprofitable." In March, 1921, the Shay arrived on a barge in Seattle "from a gold mine in Alaska." There is no documentation to prove that Lima Shay c/n 2190 was the Shay that operated at the Alaska-Gastineau, but records show c/n 2190 was built for the DEL&PCo and that it ended service with Biles-Coleman; circumstances almost certainly confirm its presence at the Juneau gold mine. From the Puget Sound Machinery Depot, in Seattle, the Shay was bought directly by the Biles-Coleman Lumber Company for use on its newly-built railway at Omak, Washington. The Shay had been converted for use with wood fuel (probably in 1913), and was almost immediately reconverted to burn coal, and in 1928 it was converted for oil fuel. The Shay was at first unnumbered, but mysteriously sported a "two-spot" plate on the smoke box when it arrived from the North. When a Heisler locomotive was bought by Biles-Coleman in 1925, it was given No. 102 while the Shay became No. 101 (in spite of retaining its "two-spot" plate). No. 101 saw less and less service, was side-lined in the early 1930s, and it is believed to have been scrapped at the Omak mill about 1940. With a final 45 miles of track, Biles-Coleman operated its railway from 1921 until 1948, scrapping the Heisler in 1949.

When Boyle leased the NLP&CCo in 1913, he also shipped in a Porter 0-4-0 locomotive (lettered DYMCo No. 3), first used in mining claims which were later included in the Canadian Klondyke Mining Company's ground (rumours say DYMCo No. 2, c/n 3023, may also have been sent to Coal Creek at this time). Porter, c/n 3024, was little used at Coal Creek however, and with the pair of 0-6-0 Porters, was abandoned at the coal-loading dock at river's edge until 1969, when three men from

| At Omak, Washington, about 1940, Biles-Coleman Shay (ex-NLP&CCo) lays awaiting the | scrappers torch, out of service for a number of years.
Eric L. Johnson Collection |

Whitehorse (Gunnar Nilsson, Harry Cooper, and Dan Nowlan) retrieved all three locomotives. None of the engines were complete, having been thoroughly vandalized over the years, but the wooden cab-work which was still on the machines was taken off before the move and left at Coal Creek. However, having been parked here for over fifty years, the locomotives had settled in the ground, and were now solidly frozen there. In the rush to extricate the Porters, the ground was blasted with explosives, damaging one (the larger) locomotive considerably. In late winter, just before the first spring thaws, the Porters were placed on skids and towed across the Yukon River and up-river to the village of Fortymile. Here they were loaded onto trucks, and freighted over Clinton Creek Road and Highway 9 (Top of the World Highway) to Dawson, and on to Whitehorse. The move took three weeks.

Dan Nowlan took the ex-DYMCo locomotive, and in 1983 sold it to Keith Christenson of Anchorage, Alaska. The larger of the pair of 0-6-0 Porters was taken by Harry Cooper, and it was eventually sold in 1992 to Dick Gilbert at Jake's Corner, although it is still located on the outskirts of Whitehorse. The smaller, more complete, of the two 0-6-0 locomotives was taken by Gunnar Nilsson. For a time it was stored behind Yukon College, but in 1993 Mr. Nilsson donated it to the Yukon Transportation Museum in Whitehorse.

DYMCo No. 2, Porter c/n 3023, may also have worked for a time on the Coal Creek railway. Its history is speculative, but rumors claim it was either swept into the Yukon River when the load-out at the mouth of Coal Creek was eroded away, or it was scrapped either at the NLP&CCo plant (unlikely) or at the Bear Creek camp. If the locomotive did indeed work at Coal Creek, it would have been after August, 1912, since one historic photo dated August 2, 1912, shows all four DYMCo locomotives at a CKMCo dredge construction site. There is some possibility DYMCo No. 2 may have gone with the Shay to the Alaska-Gastineau, since the company also acquired a few unidentified 0-4-0 Porter locomotives at this time.

The fate of many of the cars used on the Coal Creek railway is not known: there had been possibly eighteen cars bought here in 1903 (including the six from the Cliff Creek railway), two flat cars bought from the White Pass in 1909, and a few DYMCo cars brought to the thermal plant in 1913 by Joe Boyle. Some of these cars are believed to be still at the mouth of Coal Creek.

In 1937, the larger of the two Coal Creek 0-6-0 Porters is seen here at the Coal Creek landing on the Yukon River, where it was abandoned in 1918. Neither of the 0-6-0s were given road numbers. In this "Great Train Robbery" scene, the firebox has been stuffed with combustibles to produce some smoke while the "engineer", with what appears to be an R.C.M.P. cap and pistol, scans the road ahead. It would be another thirty years before this engine was recovered and taken to Whitehorse.

Yukon Archives, Claude Tidd Coll'n, 7486

Chapter 5

The Railway on Bear Creek

The Detroit Yukon Mining Company

The Canada Gazette announced that the Detroit Yukon Mining Company (DYMCo), incorporated in the state of Michigan, U.S.A., on August 27, 1902, had, on November 27, 1902, been granted a license to operate in the Yukon Territory. The syndicate was headed by Sigmund Rothschild, a cigar merchant, and Otto Brenner had been designated the Dawson agent. The company was in 1902 mining on a concession on Hunker Creek, and was preparing to mine claims 19 and 20 on Bear Creek.

A short, 36-inch gauge, railway was planned at the mouth of Bear Creek, and on July 8, 1904, four locomotives and twenty, two-ton, side dump cars arrived on the barge *Klondike* pushed by the steamer *Canadian*; four other cars had arrived earlier that summer. The equipment was said to have cost $100,000, and it had lain for several weeks at Whitehorse, held up because of unpaid freight bills. Four identical 7-ton Porter, 0-4-0, saddle-tank locomotives had been built for DYMCo in April of 1904. Given serial numbers 3022, 3023, 3024, and 3025, they were lettered D.Y.M.Co. Nos. 1, 2, 3, and 4. With 24-inch wheels, and 6x10-inch cylinders, the locomotives were of 48-inch wheelbase. The twenty-four dump cars would haul pay dirt from the company's claims down to the Klondike River where it would be washed for gold; the cars were

...of heavy iron and about ten to twelve feet long, side-dumpers, to be loaded with steam shovels...

This is mid-summer of 1904 on Bear Creek, and the Detroit Yukon Mining Company has just put one of its four Porter locomotives and a steam shovel to work, hauling gold-bearing gravel to a modest sluicing plant on the Klondike River. The right-of way snakes through the ponds and tailings at the mouth of the creek. The operation was short-lived.
Yukon Archives, MacBride Museum Collection, 3603

49

the locomotives were brand new, of the small dummy type frequently seen on suburban railways before the advent of electric railways.

In the fall of 1903, two Marion steam shovels mounted on wider gauge (perhaps standard gauge) trucks had arrived for the mining operation. The railway and shovels replaced a sluicing plant which had operated until then.

The railway operated during late summer of 1904, and during spring and summer of 1905, when the company acquired new ground. In the spring of 1905, Otto Brenner had told the press that DYMCo had purchased the Boyle Concession and was planning to bring in a "monster" electric dredge. The Boyle Concession, known as Lease 18, was huge, encompassing forty square miles of the Klondike River valley, stretching from Bonanza Creek to Hunker Creek.

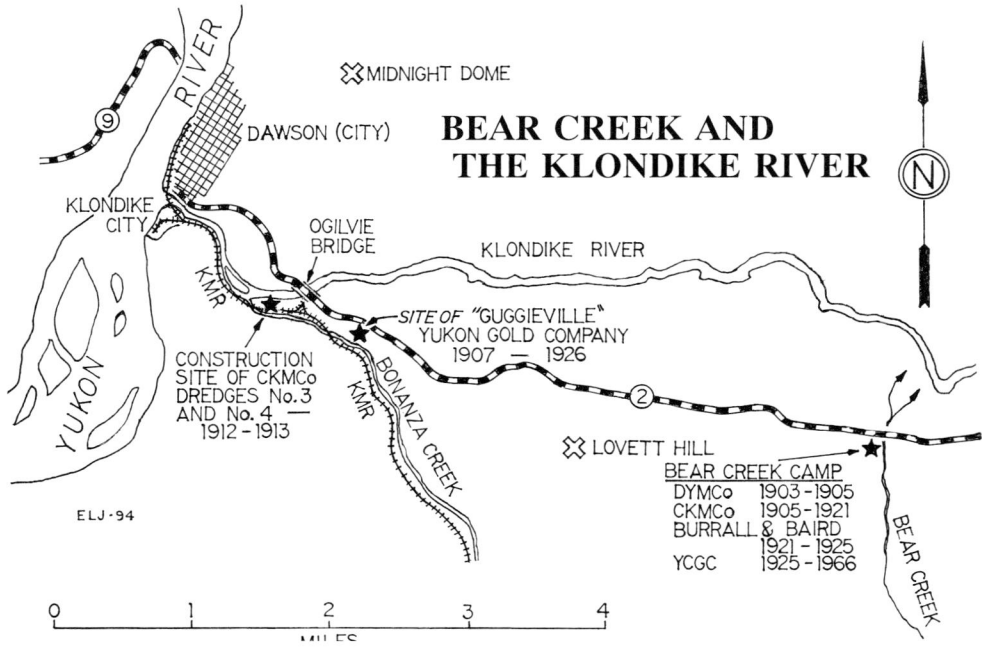

Mining gold-bearing ground at the mouth of Bear Creek in late 1904 or early 1905 is the short-lived operation of DYMCo. In the background on the 36-inch gauge track is one of the Porters and a pair of empty cars; in the foreground is one of two Marion steam shovels on the property, resting on wide-gauge track about eight feet below the haulage level. With such a shallow cut and limited production, it is not hard to see why this mining method was unprofitable. Taken over by CKMCo, these claims would be worked a year later by one giant dredge which could reach thirty feet below the surface. The dredge was capable of mining manyfold greater volumes of ground per day when compared to the steam shovels.

Environment Canada, Parks, courtesy Mrs. M. Reaney from H.A. Harms, GS 1.1-18, (neg. A-896-8)

The Canadian Klondyke Mining Company

In acquiring the Boyle Concession, DYMCo went through reorganization, and was absorbed by the newly-formed Canadian Klondyke Mining Company (CKMCo) - (in 1898 the correct official spelling for the district became Klondike). Joseph Whiteside Boyle had first gained the concession in late 1898, and later, with plenty of legal help, gained control of the CKMCo, managing it until his departure from the Klondike in 1916.

Under Boyle's direction, the company built several huge dredges, the first being operational by mid-1905, simultaneously putting DYMCo's Bear Creek railway out of work.

The four saddle-tankers were idle for a time, but found small jobs elsewhere (they were never re-lettered, carrying D.Y.M.Co. on the saddle tanks to the end). In the spring of 1909 the KMR had run a spur off its main line, just east of the Ogilvie bridge where the railway's only north end wye was located, to a tailings dump from which track ballast was hauled. This dump was at Guggieville, the headquarters of the Yukon Gold Company (YGCo), rival of the CKMCo, but DYMCo Porters may also have operated here. This spur might have been used by the Porters (when KMR trains were dedicated to hauling cordwood in the final years) to freight directly from the Dawson/Klondike City docks to the YGCo or the CKMCo dredges in the vicinity. In fact, two of the old DYMCo cars, minus dump buckets, are still on the KMR tracks in Klondike City today - trees grown around and through the frames.

When two pits, each 175 feet square and 15 feet deep, were being dug just west of the Ogilvie Bridge for the construction of CKMCo dredges numbered 3 and 4, spur lines were run to the site from the KMR mainline. All four DYMCo locomotives and the two DYMCo steam shovels are shown on the site in one historic photo dated August 2, 1912 (shown on page 55); KMR locomotives may also have worked on these spurs. In late October, about the time of KMR's annual shutdown, a large shipment of dredge machinery was landed at Dawson. Another historic photo of late 1912 (shown on Page 56) shows a DYMCo locomotive (number unknown) on KMR trackage in

At the Canadian Klondyke Mining Company's Bear Creek camp in 1905; one of the company's two Marion steam shovels has been rigged up as a crane to unload crates of parts for construction of a new dredge. In the foreground are brand new dredge buckets and a huge drive gear. Note that the shovel is mounted on trucks of greater than 36-inch gauge. On the second track is DYMCo locomotive No. 1 and the chassis of five former vee-bottom dump cars used at an earlier mining operation.

Dawson City Museum,
Dorothy White Collection,
984R-17-4-13

Dawson City; the photo is captioned "White Pass dock - hauling dredge machinery." It seems likely that the KMR had permitted the CKMCo use of the tracks for the unhurried, one mile, delivery of the dredge machinery as required during the winter for completion of construction of the two dredges.

In June of 1913 Joe Boyle shipped DYMCo No. 3 to the NLP&CCo's Coal Creek railway; it remained there until 1969. DYMCo No. 2 may also have been shipped to Coal Creek in 1913. In September of 1913 the KMR pulled up rail north of Church Street in Dawson, cutting off access to the White Pass docks, and not long afterwards the KMR bridge over the Klondike River was modified for use only by pedestrian and horse and wagon traffic. The line from Klondike City eastward however, was intact for some time after KMR shutdown, and may have been travelled by DYMCo Porters. On September 9, 1915, the Dawson Daily News spoke of another job for one of the DYMCo Porters;

> A new road is being built along the hillside between
> Bonanza and Bear Creeks, because one of Boyle's
> dredges will be working that ground. A railway track
> has been laid along the foot of Lovett Hill and a dinkey
> locomotive and dump cars have been placed there. A
> Marion shovel will be used for loading.

By the end of World War I the CKMCo was in deep financial trouble, and in 1921 was foreclosed. A private company, Burrall and Baird, Limited, took over all of the CKMCo's assets - including the remaining DYMCo locomotives (which remained with DYMCO markings and numbers over the years), dump cars, and railway equipment. By 1925 there was a great amalgamation of the major mining properties in the Klondike, and the equipment from the railway on Bear Creek, and of the KMR, all

The C.K.M.Co Construction
Camp Bonanza Basin
August The 2" 1912.

Photo By J. Doody
Dawson

In this busy scene on August 2, 1912, construction is under way on the barges which will support Canadian Klondyke Mining Company (CKMCo) dredges Nos. 3 and 4. On the temporary spurs built from the Klondike Mines Railway main line are all four of the ex-DYMCo Porter locomotives and the two steam shovels brought in by that same company in 1904. Beyond the dredge site is the KMR's wye and Old Inn station - a fair settlement has grown here. To the left is the original Ogilvie Bridge over the Klondike River, and farther away - the large buildings - is Guggieville, the camp of the CKMCo's rival, the Yukon Gold Company. The right-of-way of the Klondike Mines Railway crossed Bonanza Creek at the lower right, and they run parallel on the right side of the photo.

Yukon Archives,
MacBride Museum Coll'n, 3835

came under the control of the giant Yukon Consolidated Gold Corporation (YCGC), which would mine in the Klondike until 1966. It is believed that neither Burrall and Baird nor the YCGC operated any of the remaining DYMCo locomotives.

WHITE PASS DOCK
HAULING DREDGE MACHINERY

Although undated this photo was undoubtedly taken in late 1912, shortly after a large shipment of machinery had arrived for the construction of Canadian Klondyke Mining Company dredges No. 3 and No. 4. The locomotive is one of four the dredging company acquired in the merger with the original owner. The locomotive's presence here on Klondike Mines Railway trackage at the White Pass docks in Dawson is curious; the KMR had shut down in October, and the mining company was probably allowed use of the line for the unhurried delivery of equipment to the construction site where work was carried on through the winter. The dredge site is less than two miles from the docks.

*Univ. of Alaska Archives, Fairbanks,
Bassoc, 64-92-044*

DYMCo No. 1, c/n 3022, remained at the Bear Creek camp until 1965, when Roger Brammall of Vancouver bought the locomotive directly from the YCGC and trucked it to Whitehorse, where it was shipped via the White Pass to Skagway for final forwarding southward by boat. In Burnaby, No. 1 was stored for a time on the property of George Wood's Caribou Transport. Reputedly the best and least-used of the DYMCo locomotives, No. 1 has since the 1970s been on display, unprotected from the weather. It is located at the Whippletree Junction shopping centre, three miles south of Duncan on Vancouver Island. Brammall had superficially fixed up No. 1, painting "B.R.R.Co." on the saddle tank - Brammall Rail Road Company.

The fate of DYMCo No. 2, c/n 3023, is not known. It may have worked alongside DYMCo No. 3 on the Coal Creek railway in 1913, and it may have been scrapped there, or lost in the Yukon River; or it may have been scrapped at CKMCo's Bear Creek camp. It is also possible No. 2 left for the Alaska-Gastineau gold mine near Juneau at the same time that Coal Creek's Shay departed.

DYMCo No. 3, c/n 3024, lay derelict (thus, considered abandoned) at Coal Creek from 1918 until 1969, when it and the two CCCCo 0-6-0 Porters were recovered by salvagers and hauled to Whitehorse; over the years the three locomotives had been heavily vandalized. Dan Nowlan took possession of DYMCo No. 3, and in 1983 it was sold to railroad fan Keith Christenson of Anchorage, Alaska.

In May of 1961 YCGC donated DYMCo No. 4, c/n 3025, to the Dawson City Museum, and it was hauled from Bear Creek and parked alongside KMR locomotives Nos. 1, 2, and 3 in Minto Park. The Porter was shipped to Vancouver in early 1986, and it was then restored to original appearances by Ken Hynek of

Bonanza Basin.
May The 12. 1913.

Compare this view with that of Page 55. Now, on May 12, 1913, one dredge is nearly completed, and the other has already started to work. Most of the railway spur lines have been taken up except for those at the far end of the lot, where one Porter locomotive and a shovel still remain. The KMR's wye is now in danger of being ploughed under by one of the dredges, but in another five months the railway will be finis anyway. The wye will disappear but the main line will survive for a few more years.

Museum of History and Industry, Seattle, 9585

Surrey, B.C. During dismantling of the locomotive, Ken found many parts were missing, including a piston, hence No. 4 was probably used by CKMCo as a "parts" machine to keep others running. On display in Vancouver during Expo86, No. 4 was later returned to Dawson, and by 1987 was well-protected under the newly-built locomotive shed at the Dawson Museum site.

Two of the Porter locomotives brought to the Klondike in 1904 by the Detroit Yukon Mining Company. Last used about 1913, these two engines lay unused for many years at the Bear Creek mining camp. Taken in late 1959, this photo shows engines No. 1 and No. 4; the former is now at Duncan, B.C., and the latter in the Dawson Museum.

Environment Canada, Parks,
courtesy G. Allen Gould, GS 1.2-23

The wheels and chassis of two of the twenty-four DYMCo dump cars are still at Klondike City. Some cars were also shipped to the NLP&CCo thermal plant in 1913, and a few are said to be mired in the mud at the mouth of Coal Creek, on the Yukon River. The fate of most of the cars is unknown, although some may have gone to mines in the Mayo District.

DYMCo No. 4 was restored to new appearance for Expo86 in Vancouver, B.C. In this photo taken on June 19, 1992, it is seen back in the locomotive shed at the Dawson City Museum.

Eric L. Johnson, Vancouver, B.C.

Remnants of the Railways

The site of the railway on Cliff Creek has not been visited in years, and a survey of the rail grade and mine workings would appear to be a worthwhile heritage project. No equipment at all is believed to remain here.

On the other hand, a recent study of the Coal Creek mine site was made by Bob Mitchell and associates for the Heritage Branch of Yukon Tourism. Many decaying items of interest on site have been catalogued. While most of the twelve mile rail line leading to the mines would now be impassable, there are reports of several mine cars and flat cars mired in the mud of the Yukon River at the mouth of Coal Creek - these certainly rate a detailed examination.

At Bear Creek, no traces of the original DYMCo railway remain, dredges having so thoroughly worked over the landscape.

It is very fortunate that, of the eight locomotives brought to the Klondike for these mining railways, six still remain in existance today: one on Vancouver Island, one at Anchorage, Alaska, one at Fairbanks, Alaska, one at Dawson, and two in Whitehorse. All would doubtless have fallen to the scrapping torch years ago, had the Yukon Territory been more convenient for exploitation from the "outside". Some of the ambience of these little-known railways is still available for fans of railways and heritage.

APPENDIX A

LOCOMOTIVES OF THE INDUSTRIAL RAILWAYS

Some photographs in Appendix A are details or reductions of photographs used in the book. The credit lines are with the original photograph.

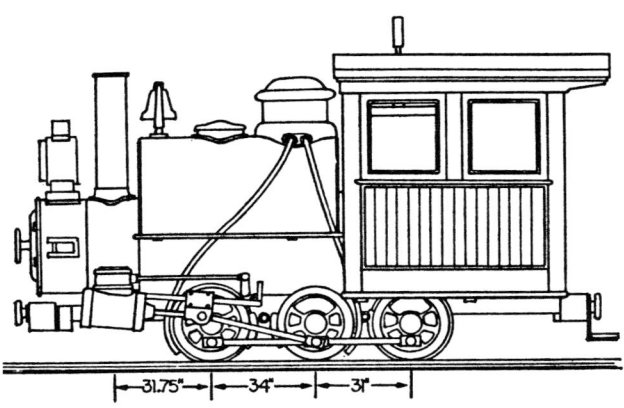

Porter (built by the H.K. Porter Company of Pittsburgh, Pennsylvania), c/n unknown, built ca. 1890, 0-6-0T, 25-inch wheels and 7x12-inch cylinders, weight about twelve tons, no lettering, no road number while in service in the Yukon.

> present owner, Yukon Transportation Museum, Whitehorse, Yukon, 1993.
> ex-Gunnar Nilsson, Whitehorse, Yukon, 3/1969 to 1993.
> exx-abandoned at the mouth of Coal Creek on the Yukon River, 6/1918 to 3/1969.
> exxx-Northern Light, Power and Coal Company, Coal Creek and Dawson, Yukon, 1909 to 6/1918
> exxxx-Sourdough Coal Company, Coal Creek and Dawson, Yukon, 1906 to 1909.
> exxxxx-Coal Creek Coal Company, Coal Creek and Dawson, Yukon, 1903 to 1906.
> nee unknown, ca. 1890 to 1903.

The smaller of two Porter locomotives which were bought by the Coal Creek Coal Company in 1903 weighs about twelve tons. After abandonment of the coal mine and railway on Coal Creek in 1918, this engine sat for fifty years on the banks of the Yukon River, heavily vandalized, and was hauled to Whitehorse in the spring of 1969. In 1993 it became the property of the Yukon Transportation Museum, seen here, in Whitehorse.

Eric L. Johnson

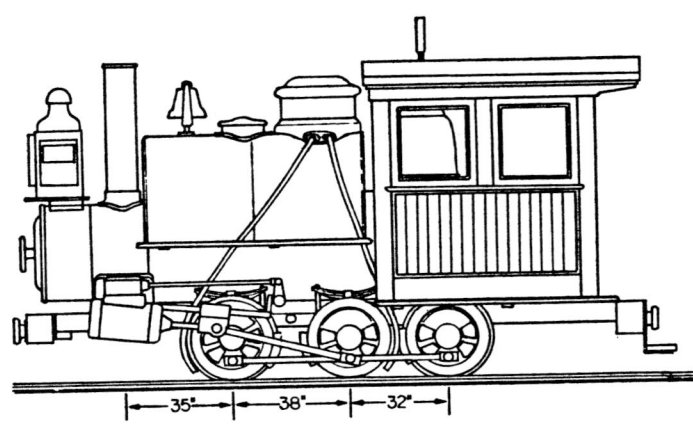

Porter, c/n unknown, built ca. 1890, 0-6-0T, 27-inch wheels and 8x14-inch cylinders, weight about fourteen tons, no lettering, no road number while in service in the Yukon.

     present owner, Dick Gilbert, Jake's Corner, Yukon (locomotive located on Venus Road, off Alaska Highway, Whitehorse, Yukon), 1992.

     ex-Harry Cooper, Whitehorse, Yukon, 3/1969 to 1992

     exx-abandoned at the mouth of Coal Creek on the Yukon River, 6/1918 to 3/1969.

     exxx-Northern Light, Power and Coal Company, Coal Creek and Dawson, Yukon, 1909 to 6/1918

     exxxx-Sourdough Coal Company, Coal Creek and Dawson, Yukon, 1906 to 1909.

     exxxxx-Coal Creek Coal Company, Coal Creek and Dawson, Yukon, 1903 to 1906.

     nee unknown, ca. 1890 to 1903.

The second engine bought by the Coal Creek Coal Company in 1903; its life story is similar to that of its mate. This 14-ton locomotive, the larger of the two Porters, is seen here in Whitehorse in 1993 - it was heavily damaged during salvaging. The construction dates, construction numbers and origins of both engines, which were built about 1890, are unknown.

Eric L. Johnson

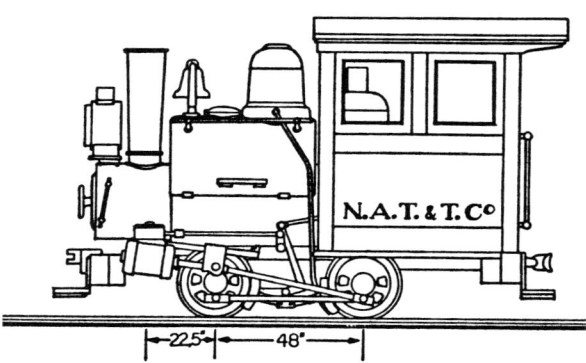

Porter, c/n 1972, built in March, 1899, 0-4-0T, 24-inch wheels, 6x10-inch cylinders, weight seven tons, cab lettered N.A.T.&T.Co., probably No. 1 while in service in the Yukon.

> present owner, Friends of the Tanana Valley Railroad, Inc., Fairbanks, Alaska, No. 1.
>
> ex-display in Fairbanks, Alaska, No. 1, from 1930
>
> exx-Alaska Railroad, Fairbanks, Alaska, No. 1, 1917 to 1930
>
> exxx-Tanana Valley Railroad, Fairbanks, Alaska, No. 1, 1907 to 1917
>
> exxxx-Tanana Mines Railroad, Fairbanks, Alaska, No. 1, 6/1905 to 1907 (n.b. TMR to TVR name change only).
>
> exxxxx-Coal Creek Coal Company, Coal Creek and Dawson, Yukon, 7/1903 to 6/1905, probably No. 1.
>
> nee North American Transportation and Trading Company, Cliff Creek and Dawson, Yukon, 3/1899 to 7/1903, cab lettered N.A.T.&T.Co., probably No. 1.

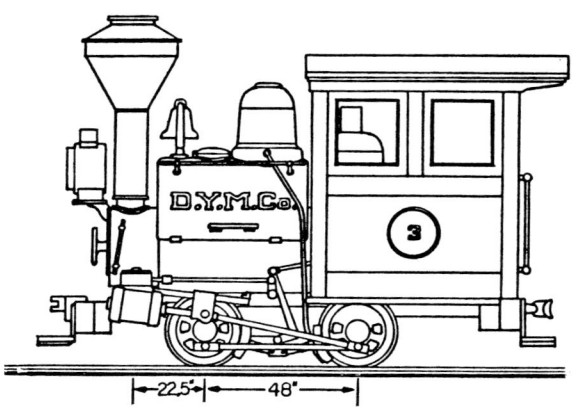

Porter, c/n 3022, built in April, 1904, 0-4-0T, 24-inch wheels, 6x10-inch cylinders, weight seven tons, originally lettered D.Y.M.Co. on tank, No. 1 on cab.

> present owner, Roger Brammall, Whippletree Junction (3 miles south of Duncan), British Columbia, 1965, No. 1, lettered B.R.R.Co. = Brammall Rail Road Company.
>
> ex-Yukon Consolidated Gold Corporation (YCGC), Dawson Yukon, 1925 to 1965, D.Y.M.Co. No. 1.
>
> exx-Burrall and Baird, Dawson, Yukon, 1921 to 1925, D.Y.M.Co. No. 1.
>
> exxx-Canadian Klondyke Mining Company (CKMCo), Dawson, Yukon, 6/1905 to 1921, D.Y.M.Co. No. 1.
>
> nee Detroit Yukon Mining Company (DYMCo), Dawson, Yukon, 4/1904 to 6/1905, D.Y.M.Co. No. 1.

DYMCo No. 1 was bought from the YCGC by Roger Brammall of Vancouver, B.C., in 1965. Brammall patched up the locomotive, repainted it, and lettered it B.R.R.Co. ("Brammall Rail Road Company") on the saddle tank. It is seen here on April 25, 1992, at Whippletree Junction, a few miles south of Duncan, B.C.

Eric L. Johnson

Porter, c/n 3023, built in April, 1904, 0-4-0T, 24-inch wheels, 6x10-inch cylinders, weight seven tons, originally lettered D.Y.M.Co. on tank, No. 2 on cab.

> fate/whereabouts of this locomotive unknown; last known to have operated in the Dawson area in late 1912, may have been: 1) scrapped at Dawson, 2) shipped to Coal Creek for use at the coal mine there and a) scrapped there, or b) lost in the Yukon River, 3) gone to the Alaska-Gastineau project near Juneau, Alaska in early 1913.
>
> ex-Canadian Klondyke Mining Company (CKMCo), Dawson, Yukon, 6/1905 to 1912(?), D.Y.M.Co. No. 2.
>
> nee Detroit Yukon Mining Company (DYMCo), Dawson, Yukon, 4/1904 to 6/1905, D.Y.M.Co. No. 2.

DYMCo No. 4

DYMCo No. 3

Porter, c/n 3024, built in April, 1904, 0-4-0T, 24-inch wheels, 6x10-inch cylinders, weight seven tons, originally lettered D.Y.M.Co. on tank, No. 3 on cab.

> present owner, Keith A. Christenson, Eagle River, Alaska, 1983, D.Y.M.Co. No. 3.
>
> ex-Dan Nowlan, Whitehorse, Yukon, 3/1969 to 1983, D.Y.M.Co. No. 3.
>
> exx-abandoned at the mouth of Coal Creek on the Yukon River, 6/1918 to 3/1969.
>
> exxx-Northern Light, Power and Coal Company, Coal Creek and Dawson, Yukon, 7/1913 to 6/1918, D.Y.M.Co. No. 3.
>
> exxxx-Canadian Klondyke Mining Company (CKMCo), Dawson, Yukon, 6/1905 to 7/1913, D.Y.M.Co. No. 3.
>
> nee Detroit Yukon Mining Company (DYMCo), Dawson, Yukon, 4/1904 to 6/1905, D.Y.M.Co. No. 3.

Porter, c/n 3025, built in April, 1904, 0-4-0T, 24-inch wheels, 6x10-inch cylinders, weight seven tons, originally lettered D.Y.M.Co. on tank, No. 4 on cab.

> present owner, Dawson City Museum, Dawson, Yukon, 5/1961, D.Y.M.Co. No. 4.
>
> ex-Yukon Consolidated Gold Corporation (YCGC), Dawson Yukon, 1925 to 5/1961, D.Y.M.Co. No. 4.
>
> exx-Burrall and Baird, Dawson, Yukon, 1921 to 1925, D.Y.M.Co. No. 4.
>
> exxx-Canadian Klondyke Mining Company (CKMCo), Dawson, Yukon, 6/1905 to 1921, D.Y.M.Co. No. 4.
>
> nee Detroit Yukon Mining Company (DYMCo), Dawson, Yukon, 4/1904 to 6/1905, D.Y.M.Co. No. 4.

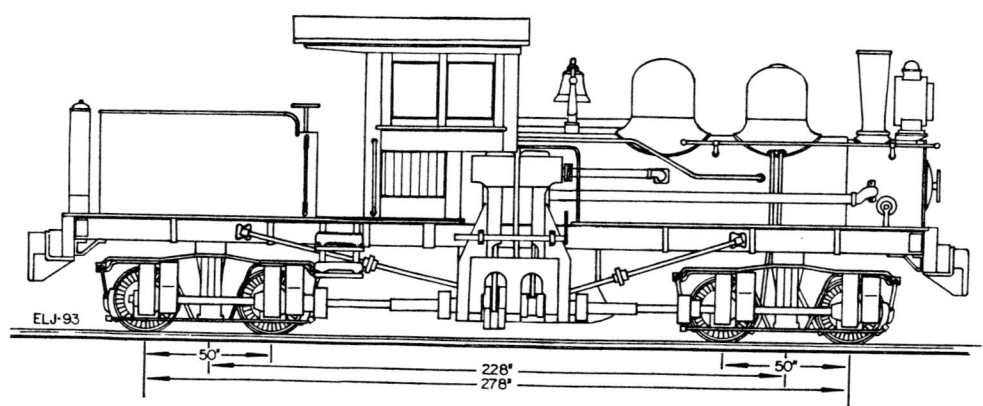

ELJ-93

Lima Shay (built by the Lima Locomotive Works of Lima, Ohio), c/n 2190, built in July, 1909, two-truck Shay, 26½-inch wheels, and two 8x12-inch cylinders, weight twenty-four tons, 10,677 lb tractive effort, may have been lettered DEL&PCo and may have had road No. 1 while in service in the Yukon. It was originally a coal-burner, converted for wood fuel in 1913, re-converted for coal in 1921, and then to oil fuel in 1928..

> last owner, Biles-Coleman Lumber Company, Omak, Washington, bought 3/1921, scrapped in 1940 at the Omak mill. Lettered Biles-Coleman Lumber Co., at first not numbered but with smoke box plate No. 2; in 1925 became No. 101 (still with front plate No. 2).
> ex-Puget Sound Machinery Depot, Seattle, 3/1921, No. 2.
> exx-Alaska-Gastineau Mining Company, Juneau, Alaska, 6/1913 to 3/1921, No. 2.
> nee Northern Light, Power and Coal Company, Coal Creek and Dawson, Yukon, 1909 to 1913,

APPENDIX B

EQUIPMENT AND FREIGHT CARS OF THE MINING RAILWAYS

North American Transportation and Trading Company - 1899

At least six wooden-hoppered coal wagons were brought to Cliff Creek in 1899; all were moved to the railway on Coal Creek in August of 1903; their subsequent disposition is unknown. It is likely that the company also had some 18- or 24-inch gauge hand-tram cars for use in the mines.

Coal Creek Coal Company - 1903

Twelve "new" coal wagons and flat cars arrived at Coal Creek in 1903, in addition to the six coal wagons just arrived from the mine at Cliff Creek. It is likely the company also brought in some underground coal cars (of gauge narrower than 36-inch), in addition to others which may have come from Cliff Creek. Today a few twenty-foot, four-axle, flat cars are said to be deep in mud at the mouth of Coal Creek today, as are some underground mine cars.

Detroit Yukon Mining Company - 1904

Twenty-four vee-bottom dump cars were brought to Dawson in 1904. The wheels and chassis of two are resting on Klondike Mines Railway track in Klondike City today, others went to the railway on Coal

Creek in 1913 and a few of these are at the mouth of Coal Creek today; the fate of rest of the cars is unknown - some may have gone to mines in the Mayo District. It is believed the two rail-mounted Marion steam shovels bought in 1904 were scrapped at the Bear Creek camp.

Northern Light, Power and Coal Company - 1909

Two thirty-foot, four-axle, flat cars (built by the WP&YR) were brought to Coal Creek in 1909 for use in hauling supplies to the power plant site; at least one of these cars is said to be at the mouth of Coal Creek today.

June 11, 1992, Klondike City; the chassis and wheels of one of the Detroit Yukon Mining Company dump cars. Six inches below the surface of forest litter are the rails of the Klondike Mines Railway's Klondike City line on which the car still rests. Here on the bank of the Yukon River the car was parked some time before 1920 - aspen trees now anchor the car in place.
Eric L. Johnson

APPENDIX C

LOCOMOTIVES OF THE KLONDIKE
MINES RAILWAY

No. 1 - Brooks, (built by the Brooks Locomotive Works of Dunkirk, New York), as Kansas Central Railroad No. 7. c/n 522, built 4/1881, 2-6-0, 41-inch drivers, 24-inch leading wheels, 14x18-inch cylinders, weight forty-one tons, KMR road number 1. Now at the Dawson City Museum, Dawson, Yukon.

No. 2 - Baldwin, (built by the Baldwin Locomotive Works of Philadelphia, Pennsylvania), as Columbia & Puget Sound Railroad No. 8. c/n 7597, built 5/1885, 2-8-0, 36½-inch drivers, 24-inch leading wheels, 15x18-inch cylinders, weight fifty tons, KMR road number 2. Now at the Dawson City Museum. Dawson, Yukon.

No. 3 - Baldwin,built 1/1899 as White Pass & Yukon Route No. 7 c/n 16456, , 2-8-0, 36-inch drivers, 24-inch leading wheels, 19 and 11x21-inch cylinders, weight eighty tons, KMR road number 3. Now at the Dawson City Museum, Dawson, Yukon.

No. 4 - Baldwin, built 3/1912 as Klondike Mining Railway No. 4. c/n 37564, 2-6-2, 37½-inch drivers, 24-inch leading and trailing wheels, 15x20-inch cylinders, weight sixty tons, KMR road number 4. Present owner, Steve Wild, Wild's (game farm), Route 3, El Reno, Oklahoma.

APPENDIX D

CHRONOLOGY

1896, Aug	-Gold discovered on Bonanza Creek, Yukon Territory.
1898	-NAT&TCo began development of a coal property on Cliff Creek
1899	-NAT&TCo built 1.5-mile railway, and made first shipment of coal.
1899	-Klondike Mines Railway granted a federal charter.
1899, Aug-Sept	- First locomotive arrives in Yukon Territory, for Cliff Creek.
1902	-Development starts on Coal Creek.
1902, Nov. 27	-DYMCo granted a license to mine gold in the Klondike.
1903, Jan. 12	-Charter granted to the CCCCo.
1903, Aug	-NAT&TCo Cliff Creek mine worked out and shut down. Rolling stock shipped to Coal Creek.
1903, Aug 6	-Two Porters arrive at Coal Creek
1903	-CCCCo coal property on Coal Creek developed and 12-mile railway installed. Last spike driven in Sept.
1903, Sept	-CCCCo buys steamer *Lightning* and barge *Margaret* from D&WHNCo.
1903, Sept 14	-First load of coal from Coal Creek arrives at Dawson
1903, Fall	-Two Marion steam shovels arrive at Bear Creek.
1904	-DYMCo installed a 1/2-mile railway on Bear Creek and began mining for gold.
1904, June	-Last shipment of coal from Cliff Creek mine.
1904, July 8	-Four Porters and twenty cars arrive at Bear Creek.
1905	-DYMCo assets acquired by the CKMCo, DYMCo mining railway shut down.
1905	-Construction of KMR began.
1905, June	-0-4-0T Porter shipped from Coal Creek to Tanana Mines Railroad.

76

1906	-Construction of 31-mile KMR rail line completed.
1906	-Assets of the CCCCo acquired by the Sourdough Coal Company, which continued mining coal on Coal Creek.
1907	-YGCo organized.
1909	-Assets of the Sourdough Coal Company acquired by the NLP&CCo, which operated Coal Creek mines and railway until about 1915.
1909, Aug 26	-Shay locomotive arrived at Coal Creek.
1910	-NLP&CCo thermal-electric plant built.
1912	-NLP&CCo Shay sent to mine in Alaska.
1913, Feb.	-CKMCo leased the NLP&CCo power plant.
1913, July	-DYMCo No. 3 shipped to NLP&CCo at Coal Creek.
1913, Oct.	-KMR shut down permanently.
1914	-NLP&CCo shut down the power plant.
1914-1915	-Last year of operation of the railway on Coal Creek.
1918, June	-Rail and some equipment of the Coal Creek railway salvaged, three locomotives abandoned at Yukon River.
1918, July	-Rail of the Cliff Creek railway salvaged.
1921	-Assets of the CKMCo, including remaining railway equipment brought in by DYMCo, acquired by Burrall and Baird, Limited.
1925	-All assets of Burrall and Baird and of the KMR acquired by the YCGC, railway equipment dispersed between 1942 and 1969.
1926	-YGCo absorbed by YCGC.
1940	-Biles-Coleman Shay (ex-NLP&CCo) scrapped.
1965	-DYMCo No. 1 sold.
1966	-YCGC quits mining operations in the Klondike.
1969	-Three abandoned locomotives on the Yukon River at Coal Creek salvaged.

Endnote

Many details of the industrial railways that operated in the Klondike, and details of the Klondike Mines Railway, are unknown. If any readers can add to the stories - or correct errors in this account - the author would be grateful for their assistance. Should company documents be known, they also would be of great value. Similarly, there must be many valuable photos of railway activity tucked away in old family albums. Anything provided me would, of course, be passed on to the Yukon Archives and the Dawson City Museum for posterity.

With thanks,
Eric L. Johnson,